Merry Christmas, Mother.

Of the dozens of books that
have come thru the library lately,
this is about the best. Although
a few of the photos of people are rather
staged, this is more than compensated
for by the high quality of the art.

Yirawala just made the news
this week by requesting a sculptured bust
of himself that the S.A. State government had commissioned
a noted sculptor to do. The fuss arose when no one
knew where the bust was.

And a Happy New Year too,

Jim & Lynne.

yirawala
ARTIST AND MAN

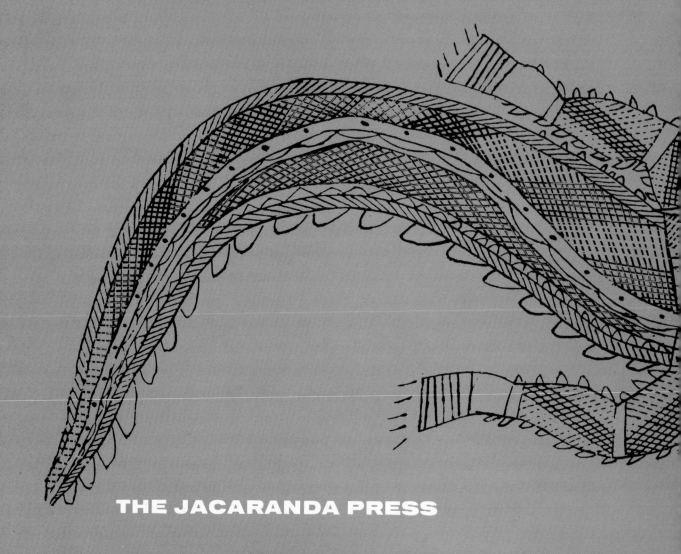

THE JACARANDA PRESS

yirawala
ARTIST AND MAN
sandra le brun holmes

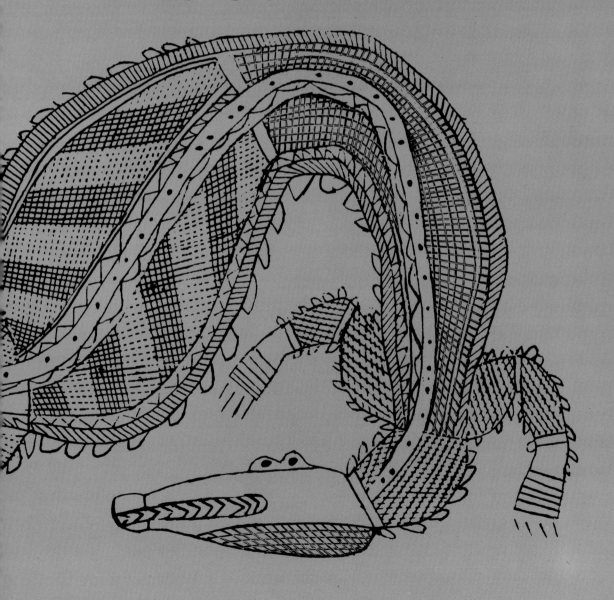

First published 1972 by
JACARANDA PRESS PTY LTD
46 Douglas Street, Milton, Q.
32 Church Street, Ryde, N.S.W.
37 Little Bourke Street, Melbourne, Vic.
142 Colin Street, West Perth, W.A.
154 Marion Road, West Richmond, S.A.
57 France Street, Auckland, N.Z.
P.O. Box 3395, Port Moresby, P.N.G.
122 Regents Park Road, London NW1
70A Greenleaf Road, Singapore 10
P.O. Box 239, Makati, Rizal, Philippines

Typesetting by Savage and Co. Pty. Ltd.
Printed in Hong Kong

© Sandra Le Brun Holmes 1972

National Library of Australia
Card Number and ISBN 0 7016 0582 0

Designed by Peter Lee

Title Page and Endpapers: Line abstractions
from photographs of two
of Yirawala's paintings.
(See pages 62 and 57)

DEDICATION

To my mother, who respected the Australian Aborigines
and was deeply interested always in their traditional life.
She permitted the women to perform some kind of ceremony
when I was a baby on our small sheep station north of
Menindee towards the Queensland border.
She said the women sang and painted my forehead.

To Emeritus Professor A. P. Elkin for his great knowledge
of the Aborigines, his profound humanity, and the
encouragement he has given me over the years to 'follow
my Dreaming'.

I humbly pay tribute to Dame Mary Gilmore, who also
encouraged me to 'go to the Aborigines, sit down and listen
to them'. Of the many great books and poems she wrote,
those about the Australian Aborigines moved me most—
and have given me strength always, in the face of adversity.

**THE AUTHOR WISHES TO EXTEND
SPECIAL THANKS TO TRANS-AUSTRALIA
AIRLINES FOR THEIR KIND HELP.**

FOREWORD

Early in 1971 at the invitation of the President of the Sydney University Union, I opened an exhibition of Yirwala's (Yirawala's) bark paintings before a large gathering which included the Chancellor and Vice-Chancellor of the University of Sydney, the Chairman of the Council for Aboriginal Affairs, several artists, some Aborigines and Yirwala himself. This, the first one-man exhibition of bark paintings, was very impressive. Incidentally, Yirwala, true to his bush custom, wore his felt hat all the time and was bare footed, but those who talked to him found him to be a dignified old man.

Some months later I was present while a small selection of Yirwala's bark paintings was shown to a committee of leading artists for their assessment, an assessment which was of no mean order. In the meantime the Queen's Birthday Honours List, 1971, announced that Yirwala had been appointed a Member of the Order of the British Empire. Further, towards the end of the year he was selected by the Committee of International Co-operation in Art, for the award of its Medallion for 1971, an award which had been made previously to leading Australian artists. As Yirwala was not well enough to come to Sydney to receive the Medallion, at his request I received it on his behalf and was proud to do so. This was on February 24th, 1972.

Yirwala, while a great Aboriginal artist, remains a great Aboriginal, and the glimpses the author of this book gives us of him personally make this clear. He does not spurn what is of use to him in the white man's culture, but his values are all based on the culture he inherited from his forefathers. At heart he is defiant of the cultural and especially of the economic flood which these days seems to be overwhelming him and the Aborigines of Arnhem Land.

Mrs. Sandra Holmes' sympathic text enables us not only to glimpse but also to feel something of the distress which is being experienced by true Aborigines. Her book is not an anthropological treatise, but an expression of the feeling and knowledge which she has gained mainly from ten years' personal experience of such Aborigines as Yirwala.

The book is enriched by the autobiographical sketches recorded by Mr. Phillip Roberts and the Reverend Lazarus Lami Lami and by the myths recorded by the latter and by Yirwala.

For their sakes after reading the galley proofs of the text (I have not seen the illustrations), and noting the author's statement that nothing in the book is of a secret nature, I readily accepted the invitation of the Jacaranda Press to write this brief Foreword to Yirawala, Artist and Man.

A. P. ELKIN
University of Sydney
22nd August, 1972

INTRODUCTION

Mr Phillip Roberts is an unassuming leader of his people. A full-blood Aborigine, who has recently received an O.B.E., he was featured in *I, the Aboriginal* by Douglas Lockwood. He was born on the Roper River Mission fifty years ago and works as a liaison officer in the Commonwealth Department of Aboriginal Affairs.

Mr Roberts's father is a 'big boss' for the Kunapipi ceremony, and for the more secret Balgin. He will inherit all the old lore from his father, and is already himself a man of influence. His status is high ceremonially and personally because he is a man of great integrity and a fighter for Aboriginal rights. He was chairman of the Northern Territory Aboriginal Rights Council, one of the few really Aboriginal organizations; this body takes up issues such as the ownership of Aboriginal Reserves, government loans for Aboriginal projects and the rights of Aborigines to have some say in their destiny.

A short resumé is included here, as an introduction to this text and to a way of life.

'I was born in the bush near the Roper River, and lived there with my parents while attending the school run by the Church Missionary Society. I went to school until I was sixteen and reached Grade Five, after which I was put out on work with the other young men. My first job was in the stock camps where I learned breaking and shoeing horses, mustering, roping, throwing and branding cattle and so on. Later on, I changed over from stock work to gardening with some of the women. After gardening, I went on to mechanical work. While doing the course in mechanical work, I took a part-time job in the Mission hospital helping the superintendent's wife with bandaging and treating sores. So my early life was taken up with hospital and mechanical work. Later I dropped the medical side and continued full time in a job with motor-cars, engines and so on.

'While all this was going on, this training in the European way of life, I still had my traditional Aboriginal training. Every year they trained me on walkabout in bush and ceremonial lore. I had to learn to accept responsibility in tribal matters. Circumcision and initiation allowed me to attend parts of our big ceremonies, like the Yubidawara and the Kunapipi. Around June, July, August was the time for the Yubidawara, and the Kunapipi would start straight after the Wet and continue for six or twelve months at a time.

'While on walkabout with my tribal family and relations, I was taught the legends of the great journeys in the Dreaming and shown the places mentioned in them, including the tribal boundaries. All these places and boundaries were fixed long ago so that each tribe had its own lands.

'The circumcision ceremony marks the transition from boyhood to manhood. Once you have borne something like that you are ready to look after a family of your own. After this ceremony was all over, everyone looked on me as an initiated man, no longer as a boy. This means that a young man can leave the camp whenever he pleases. It is something like a white boy's twenty-first birthday when he is given the key of the house and allowed to come and go at will. He can go to mixed parties and do what he likes, but with us this ceremony means separation from the girls. We were allowed to speak only with the women of the family, like mothers and grandmothers, but never with our mothers-in-law. Circumcision begins a time of testing and discipline, preparing the way for life in the tribe.

'The newly circumcized boy is not allowed to speak to anyone, man or woman, who took part in his ceremony. This silence may be enforced for five to sixteen years. If the young initiate doesn't speak to these people for the time required, they give him a present. At this, they approach the initiate and say, "I'm going to make you talk." They put their hands under their armpits and rub the sweat on the young man's lips, spreading it all over. Then they tickle him to encourage him to laugh and talk to them. After this, the younger man is allowed to talk with these persons at any time: but he is still not permitted to speak to his mother-in-law, or even to see her as long as he lives. This is the law and custom the young men must obey.

'After circumcision and the test of silence, other hardships begin for the young man. During the Lorrgon ceremony when an old man dies, the young man is burned with a fire of dry leaves or sprinkled with hot ash. These hardships must be endured before he may go through such big ceremonies as the Yubidawara, Kunapipi and Maraian.

'The young man may attend the Yubidawara after having seen a Lorrgon. He is not allowed to speak to anyone who takes part in the Yubidawara. The next step for the young man is to see the Kunapipi ceremony, and during the six to twelve months of this, the young man must learn to hunt and survive as he travels over the tribal lands. It is at this stage he is shown the tribal boundaries, and he is not allowed to speak to his parents, or even to see them. He is kept away by the elders and the Jungai-ees or leaders of the Kunapipi. This is done to train him not to depend on his parents, to train him to become a man who can look after himself, to train him to live through hardship, hunger, thirst, to train him to live outdoors under good or bad conditions through the Wet season and the Dry.

'With white children, their training starts when they go to school. They go into a building, sit on a chair at a table and are given pencil and paper. After years of this they are given a diploma, but to an Aborigine this is not enough. He must prove he can look after a wife and family and stand any hardship—and he must be able to obey the laws of the tribe.

'I belong to the Alawa tribe myself, and my proper name is Waipuldunja. When my father dies I will take over as leader of the tribe, for Gubala, my father, is the head Jungai-ee for the Balgin ceremony in our tribal area. I will one day take over from him.

'Although we Aborigines have had a lot of changes in our life, I was known as a "school boy" or a "Mission boy in the Mission paddock". When I left my school years behind, I became a man of two worlds. Although I shifted my camp from the Roper and came to live and work amongst the white men, I am still very much an Aborigine. I live in Darwin, rent a house, pay the light bills and my children go to school, but my private life and tribal laws carry on. I have a job as a liaison officer for the Commonwealth Department of Aboriginal Affairs, and I do my job just like any other public servant in a government department.

'Some people will say that an Aboriginal can be sophisticated because he has been to school and so on, but that's not right. Real sophistication is a different world. I can truly say here that I am sophisticated, in the way of living as a tribal man. I don't believe, even today in this world of change and big business in the white towns and Aboriginal Reserves, that a full grown Aboriginal person will change. The white man's influence cannot change an Aborigine from the way he lives and the way he has been taught to live, or change his culture.

'A sophisticated tribal man trying to live as a European can only do his best. No doubt in all walks of life you find struggles like this, but here in the Northern Territory, the changes are forcing the Aborigines at a pace they are not accustomed to. They are more or less living in the life of taxis, transistor radios and tape recorders, but these don't give them any future. What is the future of the Aborigines in the world of today?

'Well, I have travelled around in my work for the government departments and I have seen that although a man may be a carpenter or something on a Mission or welfare settlement, things for him do not change because he is still much in the tribal state on his tribal lands. The only way you can change the Aborigines is to give them back their tribal lands and allow them to use these in the traditional way. Then, using modern methods, help them to develop the land for themselves. Giving back their land would be giving back their pride and dignity, and this I believe will be of benefit to Australia.

'For myself, I still do not see my future as a white man does, even though I moved from the Mission and work as a public servant, because as an Aborigine my future is already made up. Although I work as a public servant from day to day I am still a tribal man. The public servant work does not give me the same pride as does the tribal life. What I am looking forward to is the day when I can return to my own tribal land, with my children and grandchildren all around me and I can say, "This is my homeland." Then I would live in pride and dignity.

'I know a number of white people, and they know me, at least on the surface. There are only two white people who I can say are true friends of the Aboriginal people, because they understand us. I am talking about Mr Cecil Holmes and his wife Sandra.

'I have known them for a number of years now, since I first met them when Mr Holmes was filming *I, the Aboriginal,* from the book of the same name by Douglas Lockwood. Since then, the Holmeses came to live in Darwin, and were always there to help the Aborigines in any way they could. We Aborigines respect these two people because of their help and understanding. We let them see our most secret ceremonies because they are trusted friends, and they have even been taken into our relationship system. Sandra is thus Jiritja moiety, Bangarditjin skin, and Karrgine (hawk) Dreaming, and Cecil is Dua moiety, Wumut skin, and Dimaia (eagle) Dreaming.

'I have checked some of the material in this book and I can say that the stories related are true, and what we people want is also true.

'It is not enough just having pretty pictures in a book like this. White people must understand how we think, what we desire, and what the land and ceremonies mean to us. These paintings are a part of our life as a whole, and may be taken as a key to the understanding of that life.'

YIRAWALA, ARTIST & MAN

In setting out to write the text of this art book, I am aware of a deep sense of responsibility to my friend of the last ten years—Yirawala.

It is my sincere hope that by reading this book and studying Yirawala's paintings and their meanings, many people will come to learn a little more about the social, spiritual, and deep ceremonial significance of Yirawala's art, for he is the last of the old cave and body painters.

Yirawala, as pictures of him within this book show, is an old Australian Aborigine, in fact seventy-eight years in 1972. He is also a man possessed of a natural dignity and an almost fierce awareness of his obligations to his people—obligations to pass on to them, through a selected male heir, the secret and sacred knowledge passed to him from his father, and from his father's father before him, and so on far back into the mists of time. This is his great responsibility, never to let the ancient Aboriginal lore die.

Yirawala paints on bark, sometimes on men's bodies for secret ceremonial rituals, and sometimes on *ranga*, the sacred wooden sticks. These sticks are hidden in sacred wells or waterholes, and only brought out by the old men for ceremonies. Sacred, prescribed designs painted on the stick, along with ancient singing, awaken the totemic spirit living in the stick. This spirit is a 'creator-being' that began the old lore, and that sanctions the ceremony itself. Even today, a mistake made in singing or in painting such objects means death.

According to Yirawala, paintings on bark walls of huts or on loose rough bark pieces were for instruction or for magical purposes, and were discarded after use. The most important paintings are in the galleries in rock caves and clefts, in which also are painted the 'title deed' designs of the tribal lands. Unfortunately for the Aborigines, these cannot be carried around, and the white man maintains that the Aborigines have no rights or titles to these tribal lands.

This book tells about Yirawala's art, and also about Yirawala the man. Some of it he tells himself, in his own picturesque way. This, and his comments on the white man's way of life, were recorded on tapes over the years.

Before bringing the reader into the complex world of Yirawala, I believe it is essential to outline something of the background of tribal Aborigines, and to note some of the social changes brought about by contact with the whites. In many cases this contact has had a fatal impact.

The Australian Aborigines differ from other race divisions of Man and so are placed in a special category, the Australoid. Scientific evidence indicates that the Australoids migrated down through South East Asia at least 35,000 years ago when the land masses were much closer together, and when it would not have been too difficult to traverse the stretches of

Far left:
A study of Yirawala with his painting of the Dreaming time giant, Lumah-lumah

Over page:
Mowani (one of four Jun-bar-bars in the traditions of Arnhem Land Aborigines) Mowani caught two girls gathering nuts in a tree in his territory. He knocked them down, killing one who was pregnant. He carried them home to eat in a dilly bag. The unharmed girl escaped and fled back to her people. Her tribe then sent four spies to seek out this horrible giant. The first two turned into an owl (Ngokaok) and storm bird (Wirriwirriyak), and the second into a bat

1

water on crude rafts. With the Aborigines came the dingo, one of the most ancient strains of dog in the world today. In Arnhem Land a few pure dingos can be seen, but a ferocious campaign of baiting and shooting dooms them to extinction in the not too distant future.

Aborigines have many stories about giant-sized men—and about more acceptable giant birds, reptiles, and other animals. These creatures have been woven into ceremonial life—like the giant snake design in etchings and paintings found in most parts of Australia. In Western Australia an old man of the Yowra tribe recorded for me the travellings of a giant emu, woven into the sacred song cycle of the Wolowolang. In fact, the footprint of this emu did exist in rock near the lighthouse at Broome, but it was cut out and taken away by an American scientific expedition. In another place on the reef near Broome, dinosaur footprints can still be seen.

Bones of the diprotodon, a giant marsupial which roamed the land about 30,000 years ago, have been found not only in Lake Callabonna, but in Aboriginal camping places, some cracked among the charcoal deposits. It seems clear that the Aborigines hunted this marsupial to extinction over a fairly short time span.

*A little boy studies his
breakfast catch*

It is fascinating to contemplate whether a deeper and more intensive
study of Aboriginal mythology could provide us with some clues about
prehistoric giants of this country.

Observing fossilized remains of animals in the Melbourne Museum,
Yirawala and his son Bobby said they had seen such things in their remote
tribal territory, inland from the mouth of the Liverpool River in western
Arnhem Land. Yirawala added that some of the bones were heavy like stones.

There are a few Australoid types living outside Australia, in Ceylon,
where they are known as the Veddas, and a few in the hills of southern
India. This seems to add weight to the scientific theory of the Australoid
migration from the north, these groups having remained behind during the
movement to the south-east. Such a migration must have taken perhaps
thousands of years.

4

It is asserted that the landfalls for the Australoids in Australia were at the top of Western Australia, in Arnhem Land, and on Cape York Peninsula. From these points they gradually spread across the whole of Australia, taking up areas of land that they call their country. These areas of land had their own natural boundaries, such as a range of hills, a stream, or a strip of desert.

The great mythological ancestors who began the ceremonial lore also created Man, plant and animal life, and the tribal boundaries. The secret rituals and ceremonies performed today perpetuate the doings of the 'creator-beings', and firmly identify Man with Nature, on which he is utterly dependent for his daily life.

Magical rituals in a nomadic existence were all-important and ensured for the Australian Aborigines the increase of the natural species of plant

George Winoguitj demonstrates the use of the old hand net. He was narrowly defeated as an Independent in recent Legislative Council elections. He seeks to limit foreign capital in the Northern Territory

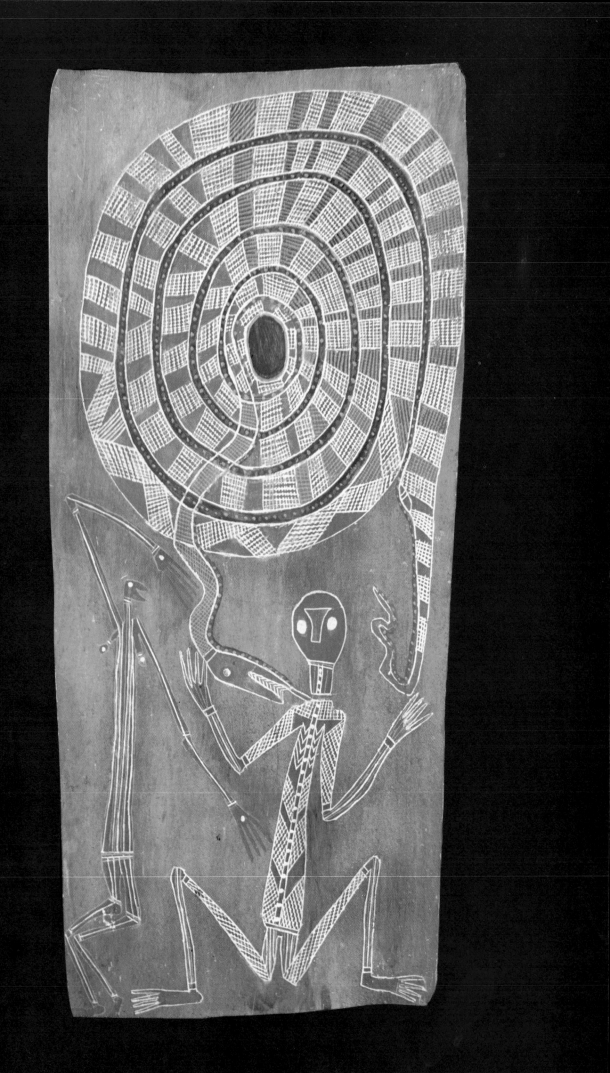

and animal life upon which they depended. Such rituals could only succeed if performed correctly, hence the severe punishment for a mistake.

In caves there are 'increase' drawings of fish, birds, mammals, and reptiles. A man may sing and paint one of these in the belief that it will succumb more easily to his club or spear; such drawings could be painted one on top of another. Ceremonial type drawings, ancestral hands and totemic signs were left intact. These were 'power' designs and were equivalent to clan title deeds to their tribal territories. Certain old men are keepers of these 'power' caves; one such man is Yirawala. He is responsible for protecting them from desecration, and for retouching drawings of significance and repainting human remains, particularly skulls.

One very secret 'power' cave of which Yirawala is guardian is the Lumah-lumah cave, wherein the bones of the great giant who began the Maraian ceremony are said to rest. No man except the keepers of such places would dare go near them for fear of death: men call such a place a 'danger place'. It is said by Yirawala that evil will also befall any white man who profanes these places. Yirawala and another old man, Paddy Compass, believe that if the caves are desecrated physically, or revealed in published photographs to all and sundry, the tribes will perish.

In fact, old men have actually given up the will to live once they are moved from their 'power' places, for these are sacred objects which to them generate all life and hope for the future. Where white people have destroyed sacred places and objects, the ceremonies associated with them die out, and demoralization of the people soon follows.

Skinning a dugong on Elcho Island. This marine mammal yields a highly prized meat much like beef. It has breasts like a woman and holds its feeding young with its flippers. Although protected, its numbers are seriously depleted

Far left:
Nowyran, the giant snake, biting the head off a bad child who was always whining. The mother tries to fend off Nowyran in vain. All naughty children have much to fear from the giant snake

7

The attack on the mosquito-people. The people of the mosquito clan lived during the Dreaming time in the mangrove swamps at a place called Morgaleetbah about eighty kilometres inland from the mouth of the present day Liverpool River. They built conical huts out of pandanus palm poles and bark. A single hole at the top of the cone served as a doorway and as a chimney for the smouldering fire always kept on hand. One fateful night, three huge pythons attacked the clan in their huts, killing most and scattering the survivors

8

It is extremely sad that even today, few white people recognize or understand that the Australian Aborigines have their own religion, closely linked with their art and economy. In fact all is a single skein. To destroy one is to destroy all, for the drawings are parts of the great religious myths, and in the absence of writing such drawings and etchings tell stories and are a record of the tribal history.

The Australian Aborigines have no religious affiliations with any other tribes around them, as in their own areas are all their 'power' places from which, according to their beliefs, come life and all sustenance. The clan waterholes contain ancestral and totemic beings. From there comes the spirit child to its human mother, and after death, prescribed ritual ensures that the spirits of the dead return to the clan waterhole.

Most of the Aborigine's traditional life is secret, and his thinking revolves, in the main, around the ceremonial life, the economy which depends on that ceremonial life, and the designs that illustrate and perpetuate it. A fully initiated man carries in his head songs, ritual acts, and painting designs enough to fill volumes—apart from an intimate knowledge of the seasons, of the movements of birds, reptiles, fish and mammals, of the seasonal ripening of certain nuts, bush fruits and vegetables necessary for a basic day to day survival.

The Australian Aborigine is remarkably well adapted to his own bush environment, but finds the white man's world with its very very different values shattering and difficult to comprehend.

Before we rush to dub them as a shiftless, irresponsible lot, let us please consider how different their experiences, background, and environment are.

An Arnhem Lander demonstrates the art of throwing a spear using a woomera. This formidable weapon was once used against invading white men

Far right:
Bolig-bolig the 'sugarbag' man. This spirit man has a great love of sweet things. Wild honey or 'sugarbag' is collected from hives in trees and logs and rock crevices. Also, a fine white sugary powder is laboriously gathered from the surface of certain leaves. This sweet powder disappears when the sun warms it, so it must be gathered very early in the day. When there is little powder to be had, the Aborigines say that Bolig-bolig has beaten them to it

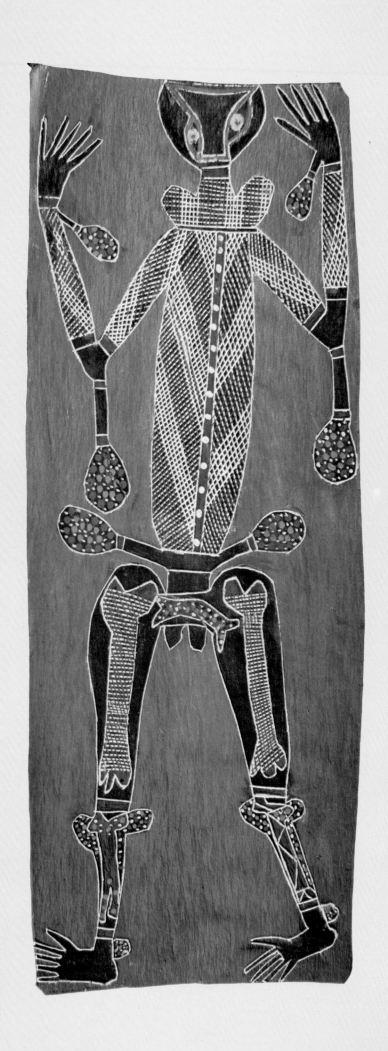

Maralaitj, the creator-ancestress of the northern tribes. Ngarljod the snake of the rainbow, brought Maralaitj two husbands after she was blown from the direction of Indonesia. At the Gargoiyang waterholes in Gunwingu country Maralaitj gave birth to the tribes, assigning the classificatory relationships that gave the tribes their social cohesion. She is now said to live at the end of the rainbow (association with Ngarljod)
Left: Maralaitj giving birth to the tribes
Centre: Jiritja moiety divided into 'skins' by Maralaitj
Right: Dua moiety divided into 'skins' by Maralaitj

Our values are mainly monetary, theirs were, and in some cases still are, purely spiritual—tied up until death with their land and religion.

Most white people who do not trouble to do their homework on the Australian Aborigines look upon them as an inferior, brainless people. If one stops to think, any man who is bi-lingual, speaking English and the Aboriginal tongue, remembers an enormous number of tribal songs, dances, paints designs, and can live off the land, is anything but stupid. He merely thinks differently from the white man.

The Aborigines had remained unconquered and undisturbed until white settlement began in 1788. Massacres of Aborigines throughout Australia are legend now. In some areas, where today big cities rear their polluted heads, the local tribes were poisoned or shot out like rabbits. For a single white man killed, a whole tribe would be wiped out. They were not regarded as being human, and even today many whites have reservations about their mental ability.

It is clear that in his own environment the Aborigine of Australia is sophisticated—though he is not in ours. In turn, a white man is most unsophisticated if suddenly forced to live in the bush. Imagine a white man

12

Yirrkala dancers performing for visitors on 'open day' at the Bagot Welfare Compound about four kilometres from Darwin. Whites are usually forbidden entry

learning the Aboriginal language quickly, not breaking their laws, being forced to adopt their religion—being forcibly assimilated by the Aborigines, instead of vice versa.

Yirawala understands the white man's acquisitive world well enough and takes from it what it can give—except the Christian religion and the dull acceptance of assimilation. Like many, he has the 'tree of fruit' philosophy about our world: when the fruit runs out or is sour, he moves on.

Yes, he, like others of his people, will take all he can from the *balanda* (white man), for in his heart and mind he does not forgive or forget the wrongs done by whites.

I do not think that any Aborigine loves white people. Why should he? Even so, the bitter 'fruit' he now eats is poisoning him slowly but surely. He has no political understanding (I am speaking of the unsophisticated full-blood here), and little understanding of the white man's world. Anyway, on Missions and settlements his thinking is done for him and rarely is he asked: 'What do you think?' or 'What do you want to do?'

In the Northern Territory, he has been in institution-type Missions and government settlements which have been, and to a large extent still are.

13

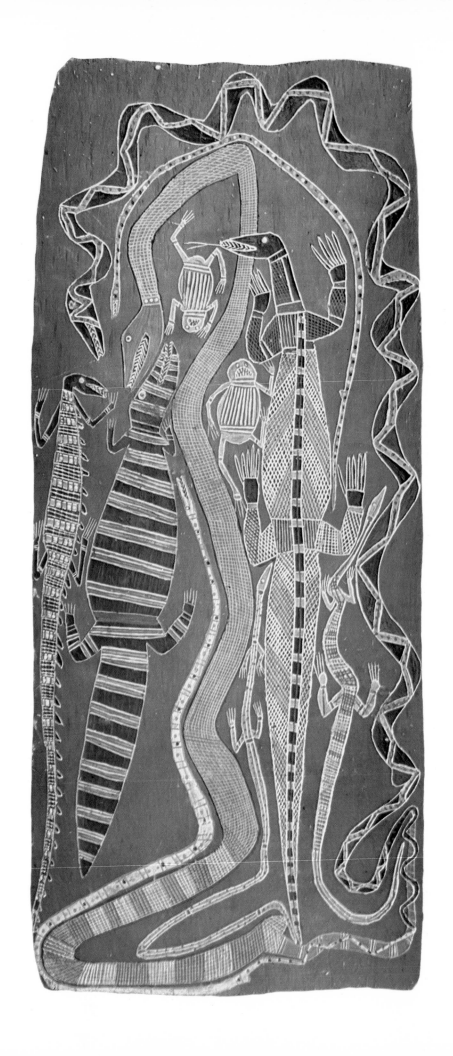

Millingimbi men 'on show' for visitors on 'open day' at Bagot Welfare Reserve

Far left:
Healing magic painting. Daadbi the venomous snake and Guluwan the goanna fighting. Daadbi wanted Guluwan's house, but the goanna put up such a fight that the snake was beaten. Guluwan healed the many dangerous bites he received by rubbing his excrement and spittle into the punctures. Goanna excrement and liver are used by the Aborigines to treat venomous snake bites. This painting depicts venomous snakes and goannas associated with healing magic for snake bite. Yirawala is a medicine man of prestige among the Gunwinggu and other nearby tribes

paternalistic. Until recently he was given a weekly handout which adversely affected his pride, dignity, and sense of responsibility. One might well turn to these 'powers that be' and say: 'Look upon your work.' What works of woe for the indigine, to be sure!

Today, with inroads made by mining companies, without protection for sacred caves and sites, and so far without land of their own by our law, the Aborigines are drinking and fighting, and there is a monthly sprinkling of assaults and killings. On some settlements, they have introduced wet canteens, presumably to teach the indigenes how to drink. There is undeniable evidence that as a result, drinking and drunken fighting are on the increase: people who have never had access to alcohol now have a canteen to go to, and often whetted appetites lead to quantities of hard liquor being brought in from outside, with disastrous consequences.

Under all these stresses the indigenes are breaking down. Yirawala says that only returned tribal lands and cash loans for enterprises can save the people now.

The Arnhem Land Aborigines are believed to be one of the most primitive of peoples remaining, so a very brief outline of their social organization is worth tracing here.

Each tribe is divided into two halves, or moieties. One half is called the 'Dua' moiety, and the other, 'Jiritja'. All the species of bird, plant, and animal life, and all inanimate objects are similarly classified—so Man and

Nature are closely allied. Objects of the appropriate moiety classification
are often traded or given as gifts to close friends or relatives. Rights to
moiety objects are rigorously defended. Traditional painters, like the other
members of a tribe, belong to one moiety or another, and paint only the
designs of things in that moiety.

In Arnhem Land, each moiety is divided into four divisions called 'skins'.
Other Australian tribes tend to use a 'two skin' system. The double tribal
system of the Northern Territory allows for a greater number of related
people. Each skin has its own name. Each person, besides having a moiety
and skin name, also has another classification name, called a 'Dreaming'
thing or object. Yirawala's is Dadat, the red and green parrot of the region.

The Aboriginal social classifications were designed to ensure the orderly
survival of the tribe. Under this system, a person's relationship to any other
in the tribe is known. This is important because relationship governs
behaviour towards one another, social status, marriage, social obligations
and privileges. These classificatory relationships, governed by the ancient
kinship laws, tend to 'breed out' disease and disability. They ensure the
provision of defence and care for the weak, the young, and the aged.

16

Both maternal and paternal lines of descent and inheritance are variously used under the kinship laws. Although intricate and incomprehensible to the white man, the kinship laws remain workable for as many as fourteen hundred people. The elders who administer these laws and pass judgment according to them, know each person as an individual, and do not have to rely on complex tables and formulae to arrive at the appropriate relationship. Any breaches of kinship laws meant death in times past, and today still carry stern disapproval.

Polygamy worked in the traditional Aboriginal life, though frowned on by the white missionaries. When a girl is born, her father arranges a marriage promise with an older man of the opposite moiety and the correct skin. This arrangement binds the two families in mutual support, the son-in-law being especially responsible for the father of the girl. A man might have two or three promises or wives, which gives him greater influence because he can look to a greater number of people for support in times of stress. Also, the preparation of large amounts of food during ceremonies makes wives definite assets.

Adultery was traditionally frowned upon, and sometimes punished with death. Genuine affection is common in these marriages. If a wife deserts her husband, both families strive to effect a reconciliation. Should this fail, the deserting wife and her family must compensate the wronged man with valued items, sustenance, and support.

The division of labour between the sexes is clearly defined, as is the ceremonial life, though some of the latter is shared. The men control almost all ceremonials and all the kinship laws, as well as the sacred objects which no woman may see on pain of death. In any case, a woman would not want to know anything of these, as they are none of her concern and are fraught with danger. In some cases, women have their own ceremonies secret from the men. These are mainly associated with a young girl's coming of age. Some are associated with ancestral heroines, but tend to emphasize the role and functions of women. In female ceremonies, and in things like love magic, certain of the older women have powers above the others, like the male elders.

The classificatory relationships and ceremonial life of the Aborigines are interwoven with associations with the tribal lands. Even the language is involved, and the whole forms a religious fabric that varies from one tribal land to another. Within the tribal boundaries are power places, spirit places and increase places associated with the origins and religious life of the tribe. The spirit of each member of a tribe pre-existed in one or another of these spirit places, and returns there when the human body dies. Hence, a man's tribal land or country is his spiritual homeland as well.

If we study these aspects of the Australian Aborigine, their thinking processes and their ceremonial lore, we must conclude that interference destroys their whole social fabric. Even though they will accept our goods and money and even attend our churches—often with little option—this does not change their real, inherited traditions and set of values, which are so different from ours.

In the Northern Territory, many anthropologists have done important work for the Administration and for the Australian Institute of Aboriginal Studies. The gaining of this information, however, does not ensure the survival of this way of life. Yirawala and others like him prefer integration to assimilation, hoping their ethnic group can preserve its unique identity and still benefit from the modern technology of the white man.

It is against our law today to shoot and poison Aborigines, but with the loss of their land, religion and social organization, the consequent loss of their identity will destroy them in time. Breakdown of the kinship laws means a breakdown of the complex and effective social organization. From the seed of this breakdown we reap a hideous harvest of alcoholism, prostitution, drunken violence, and the neglect of children, widows and the aged.

Closing off access to alcohol would remove many of these problems, but scientists who have studied Aborigines and their traditions know well that degeneration and demoralization are the result of loss of dignity, pride, self-reliance, and of being more or less cooped up on missions and settlements.

The Aborigines of Oenpelli now fear for their sacred places, the pivot of their lives. Many also now know that despite the fact their lands are declared reserves, they seem to be reserves for the white man's exploitation. They know they own not one acre, according to our law.

Despite heavy odds, Yirawala has fought back. He has never pretended to be a Christian for material gain. In truth, he despises the people trying to foist alien beliefs and laws on to his people. Yirawala is truly one of the last real men of courage and integrity, still hoping to keep back the tide of mines and men invading his country. He fears for the sacred places, and says he wants my help to get good white people to help him. I refrained from voicing my doubts and fears in the face of his resolve and strength of purpose.

He eventually put me through a short ceremony between the two of us, to give me the 'power of the tongue', as he put it. He said I must have more power in order to help him and his people. I think only changed government policy could help.

I first met Yirawala about ten years ago when I accompanied my husband Cecil to Arnhem Land, travelling up from Sydney for the purpose of making films for the Methodist Overseas Mission, the A.B.C., and the Australian Institute of Aboriginal Studies. The first stop was Goulburn Island, and there Lazarus Lami-Lami of the Maung people first told me about Yirawala and of his greatness as a painter and ceremonial leader. Lazarus, who is now an ordained minister and an M.B.E., said that before I went to see Yirawala he would tell me some Maung stories well known to Yirawala (a Gunwinggu), as some of the mythology was linked. He also said that Yirawala originally came from an area east of Oenpelli, on the edge of the escarpment country where the Liverpool River peters out, that he had lived on Goulburn for a time, and that he was now on Croker Island.

One of the Maung stories was about a big man, like a giant, whose name was Wadakak, sometimes called Wurrugag. The giant's Dreaming thing was 'stone', and he was of the Nagila skin. Wadakak's trouble started near the Alligator River. He wanted a girl for a wife, but she was in the wrong moiety and skin for him. The girl's relatives wanted Wadakak to leave and look elsewhere for a wife. He wanted the girl very much, and thought often of the pleasure of taking her to wife. However, his fear of being killed was stronger, so he set out along Cooper Creek, walking all night and sometimes pausing to think of the girl.

During the night, Wadakak passed close to the camp of another tribe, the Yirdu. Next day, the old men of that tribe found out from the younger men that Wadakak had no woman with him. They were worried, knowing that the big man was woman-hungry and might come to them, perhaps to

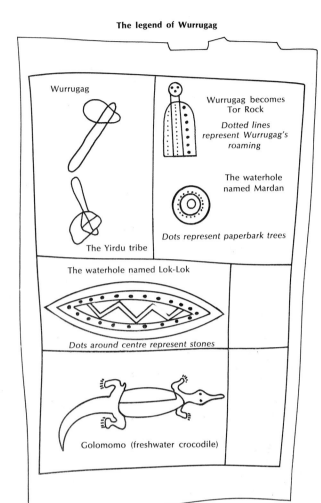

Wurrugag

Wurrugag becomes
Tor Rock

*Dotted lines
represent Wurrugag's
roaming*

The waterhole
named Mardan

Dots represent paperbark trees

The Yirdu tribe

The waterhole named Lok-Lok

Dots around centre represent stones

Golomomo (freshwater crocodile)

steal a woman. So the old men ordered that the tribe's waterhole be covered with paperbark and branches as a strong warning to Wadakak that he must move on from Yirdu tribal lands.

When Wadakak found the covered waterhole of the Yirdu he roared with rage, vowing vengeance but not daring to remove the cover. He wandered on, seeking to slake his thirst, and soon came to a waterhole called Lok-Lok. Feeling weak, he leaned far over the water and thought how cool it was. Through its clear depths he could see many fresh-water crocodiles. He was quick to see there were many female crocodiles down there, and that all seemed very happy.

After drinking deeply, the big man stood by the waterhole watching the happy reptiles, and a great sadness came upon him. Through tears of loneliness he said to them, 'I call you Golomomo, and you are my Dreaming thing now.' Weeping and sighing, Wadakak wandered slowly on. He came to a flat expanse, and there raised his arms and sang his last song before turning himself into the mighty Tor Rock. It remains a landmark for many

Left:
Painting telling of the travels of Wurrugag

Right:
Explanation of Wurrugag painting

19

The author and Yirawala on the beach at Croker Island

miles around in the coastal region of eastern Arnhem Land, on the way to Millingimbi.

Another man, Winunguitj by name, added some more to the story of Wadakak.

Wadakak was once promised a wife of his own, a young and comely girl named Wadamudunguiji; but she did not want him because he was fat and his size frightened her. The young girl and her family lived at a place called Mangulkarrn, and it was here she first menstruated. Her father built a shelter for her in which she was secluded with her mother and a few older women. The girl did not voice her fears to her mother, but helped her to scoop out a sleeping hollow in the sand. The sand they pushed out for the hollow became two sand hills. When her mother was asleep, Wadamudunguiji crept away and sat down on a stone, worrying and trying to think of a way out. She raised her tear-stained face to the empty sky and cried for some answer, but no answer came. So she wandered on and on until she came to a place called Paniwilngukukuk. She knew she could never be wife to

20

Wadakak, and so in final despair she chanted magic words and turned herself into a stone.

This story is part of the old Maung mythology and is linked with a ceremony called the Ninji. I saw part of it on Goulburn Island, when Winunguitj interpreted for me the bringing out of a young girl from seclusion. Her father had painted her face with intricate designs and then led her out from her seclusion, beating heavy clapsticks and singing. Her mother came out with her, similarly painted, while a male relation played the didjeridoo.

About the time I met Lazarus, he had been asked by the Mission to take up residence on Croker Island to assist in his capacity as a fully trained carpenter, and later to study for the ministry. So it was that Lazarus was able to introduce me to Yirawala.

Croker was much bigger than I had expected, and the track from the airstrip near the sea wound through miles of well watered, verdant grazing country, dotted here and there with groups of fat cattle and the beautiful

Yirawala with part of his family on Jap Creek, Croker Island. Margaret is at the rear, Mary in front. His son Andrew is too preoccupied to notice the camera

21

blue-grey dancing brolgas. These birds are of the crane family, as tall as a man, and have a graceful gliding stride as they move over the plain in family groups. The Mission houses dotted hillocks overlooking sweeping white beaches and dazzling blue sea, a great contrast to the grey sand beaches of Darwin. Here there were white-crested waves, not the oily flat calm of Darwin's harbour. It was truly a beautiful place.

As we walked down to the beach camp where Yirawala lived with his two wives and children, my heart lifted at the sight of Jap Creek, with its milk-white sand set against a red cliff and olive-green mangrove trees. It is a crystal clear tidal creek, with colours of blue and green beautifully mingled.

In the shade of a clump of pandanus palms sat the old man, a hat on the back of his head and part of a pipe in his mouth. Next to him lay a couple of skinny, nondescript dogs. Behind the patch of shade stood a rough hut made of bark and pieces of sheet iron.

Lazarus and I sat down a few feet from the old man, who looked up at us with penetrating eyes. He nodded his fine old head and resumed his intricate painting on a piece of bark lying across his knees. Presently, he completed the section he was working on and laid it aside, his hands as steady as a surgeon's. He smiled and held out a slender hand with extremely long nails. We shook hands and smiled, and Lazarus made the introduction in a dignified manner, his voice deep and resonant. In his shorthand English Yirawala asked me the purpose of my visit. We hit it off well, and were soon deep in conversation, now serious, now laughing. I found he had a rather sardonic sense of humour.

After some days in close contact with Yirawala I realized that what Lazarus and others had told me was true. Here was the last of the true cave artists, from a long line of such men: men who were also top ceremonial leaders of the Gunwinggu people. I was amazed at the greatness evident in his art, at its beauty, movement, and the great skill in handling. Most important of all, the designs closely resembled those I had seen in the caves of Arnhem Land. Here was the master, and mentally I called him the Picasso of Arnhem Land; for like Picasso, Yirawala is a burning patriot of his people and land, courageous, uncorrupted, and a great artist.

Yirawala complained to me of the Missions. They did not seem to understand his art, did not understand that selling it piecemeal broke up the 'story' he was telling. He was concerned that his 'story' would be lost or broken up. He said he wanted me to take his paintings and keep the important ceremonial works in series. Up until then, the Mission had bought all works for resale to dealers. Failing eyesight and advanced age mean that the whole series will not be done again.

The Reverend Jack Goodluck of the Methodist Mission on Croker Island was an extremely helpful, Christian man, but was transferred to Darwin. The people were very sorry to see him go. When he left, the new manager and Yirawala did not see eye to eye and not all of the important paintings were sent on to me as we had planned. When Yirawala found out, he was very angry and wanted to come to Darwin to paint, so that I would be able to keep the series intact. Unlike most of the Aborigines, Yirawala will stand up to white authority when he knows he is right.

When I sat talking to him at our first meeting I could not realize that our association would become such a strong bond. I can recall him on that first day, alert and laughing as he shouldered his little son Andrew while his two attractive young wives brought food and drink. There was the firelight's

23

Maraian white barramundi, first seen and named by Lumah-lumah, one of the most important of the Dreaming time giants. He classed it as sacred, and created a dance and a song to honour the fish. The dance as it is performed today suggests fish swimming and the motion of waves

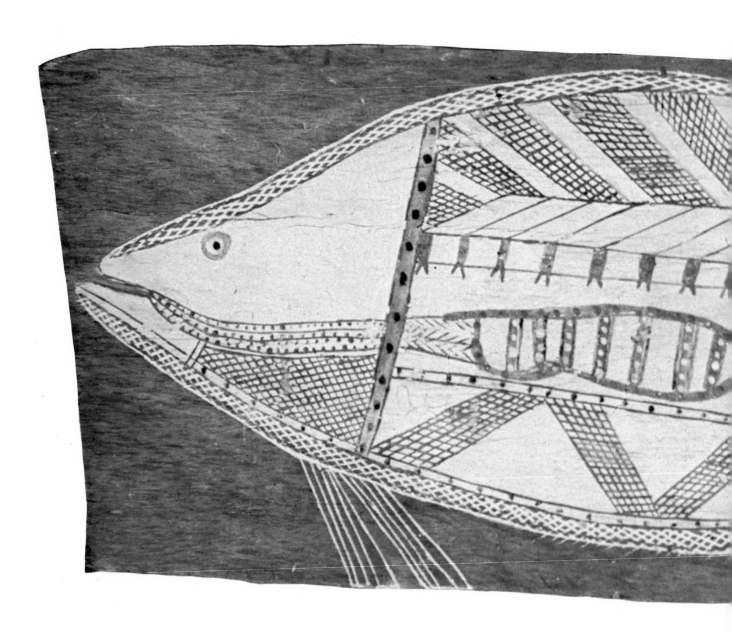

24

Yirawala and his friend Mijau-mijau show how the walls of a bark hut were sometimes painted in the old days. Kangaroo figures are Kundaagi, the red plains kangaroo, common to the Maraian, Ubar and Lorrgon ceremonies. The artist signs the painting by placing hand and arm against the painting surface and blowing paint to form a silhouette

glow on the old man's intelligent face, and the aroma of geese roasting in the paperbark ovens made by his wives, Margaret and Mary. They made the ovens by scooping out hollows when the fire died down, lining them with hot stones, and placing the plucked and cleaned geese wrapped in paperbark inside. Around this was placed more paperbark in the shape of a pot-bellied chimney, the top of the 'chimney' protruding above the heap of hot stones, coals, and ash.

Yirawala talked of his first wife when he was a young man. She had died after bearing three children, two of whom are now over forty. Mary had given him two sons, Bobbie Jorron and Danny, twenty-six and eighteen years respectively now. Margaret presented him with little Andrew, now eleven. Yirawala has always been a good and loyal husband, father and provider. Of his sons, only Bobbie and Danny may learn his secret designs, and then only when they are 'grey-haired', or fully initiated.

Before I left Croker Island, Yirawala invited me to record part of the sacred 'white fish dance' from the Maraian ceremony, which cannot be published.

26

Women of Croker Island cooking geese. Wrapped in paper bark and baked slowly, these water fowl make a delicious and tender dish

It was when walking back to the Mission with Lazarus from the first meeting that the idea of a book to assist white people to understand the Aborigines and their culture and mythology came to me. Stopping by Lazarus's house, I asked after a pair of Muscovy ducklings I had given him previously as a gift. He replied with a sigh that he had followed the instructions for housing them a little too literally and had built their little house too well. Some visiting relatives had moved into it. But Lazarus was of great assistance as an interpreter, especially with the Maraian fish dance, which I recorded for the Australian Institute of Aboriginal Studies. Yirawala did a bark painting segment of this fish dance to accompany the recording. The Institute would not buy the piece, but an ethnomusicologist, Mrs Moyle, who is a Research Fellow for Monash University, finally agreed to take it. Yirawala showed me how he had painted a segment of the Maraian before I left Croker Island. The deftness of his stroke and the beauty of design amazed and delighted me.

By this time my husband Cecil and I had moved to Darwin, where he worked on a magazine called the *Territorian*. When he had time, he made

Portrait of Yirawala at the Dripstone Caves

anthropological films for the Australian Institute of Aboriginal Studies. Sometimes I assisted with sound, continuity and some documentation. The Aboriginal headmen trusted us and permitted us to film and document secret ceremonies, and their trust was not betrayed.

According to Yirawala, the Mission management did not take too happily to his attempts to market his paintings independently. Before he came to Darwin, he had sent by boat a bundle of blank bark pieces for new work. A telephone call to the Mission warehouse in the town did not yield any information on Yirawala's parcel, which he was sure had arrived. We went to the warehouse and there he found his parcel. A white employee first opened it and examined each sheet before we were allowed to take it. Yirawala said that it was to ensure that he had not tried to remove from the Mission any works he had done while living there. Further difficulties like this followed, and finally Yirawala, with the help of a lawyer, more or less contracted to give me right of first refusal, with him setting the price. This has worked well over the last three years, in spite of the financial strain. The more important ceremonial pieces were a series covering the main part of the Maraian ceremony, with shorter segments of the Lorrgon and Ubar ceremonies. My deepest regret is that a full series of the Ubar intended for me was lost to a visiting dealer, but this was before the legal agreement.

28

Old men from Millingimbi enjoy a smoke from a long-stemmed copper-bowled pipe. This type of pipe was first introduced long ago from Indonesia.

So that series was probably broken up and sold by the sheet, God knows where. . . . The tragedy is that Yirawala is now too old and ill and poor-sighted to repeat that series.

Lazarus Lami-Lami, the man who introduced me to Yirawala, came to Darwin every few months with much material collected for me to tape. We even corresponded by tapes—'talking letters', as the people called them. On one such visit, Lazarus told me of his own background, which is interesting to include to give the reader an idea of a way of life. Taken from tapes, his story is reproduced here in his own words.

'I was born on the mainland opposite Goulburn Island. There we lived off the land, which was rich in game, and the seas were filled with shellfish, crayfish, ordinary fish, and dugong, just to name a few. From hollow tree branches and the ground we collected "sugerbag", or wild honey made by little black bees, more like flies to look at. Unlike the bees which make honey for the white man, ours have no sting.

'Our blankets were made of cabbage palm bark, and the pandanus palm provided mats. We made dilly bags of all kinds from the pandanus palm. Some were so fine that they could carry honey. Cabbage palm made good square baskets, often used for water. For cups we used a twist of paperbark, a large leaf, or just a cupped hand.

'As children, we loved to pick wild plums, grapes, nuts, and berries. And best of all was to dive into a lagoon for lily roots and later to roast the seed pods.

'We all used piles of paperbark, with sharp sticks thrust through to hold them together, to cross lagoons, to fish from, or to hold things on when crossing creeks. We also used bark canoes.

29

Potsherds of Indonesian origin collected from the sea and beaches along the coast of Arnhem Land. Drying ovens, ballast stones and tamarind trees are further evidence of the early Indonesian visitors who came for trepang, mother-of-pearl and tortoise shell

Far right:
The mother of Kundaagi. Paintings concerning the Kundaagi legend indicate dances in the Ubar, Lorrgon, and Maraian ceremonies

'It was the early sailors from Macassar—you call them Indonesians— who taught us how to make the dugout canoe which was a blessing to us, as with them we could go on sea voyages and spear big sea turtles and dugong; we could not do this with the frail bark canoe. These men first came from Macassar to the shores of Arnhem Land maybe a few hundred years ago, and I can remember them as a boy, before the white man began patrolling the coastline to keep them out. They came to dive for trepang and pearl shell and for tortoise shell which they valued highly. Our people had trade agreements with them, and the old men say they always honoured them. The Aborigines helped them with the trepang, and even learned the exhausting curing process. These Indonesian visitors introduced the long-stemmed pipe, among other things. Our people got on well with them, for they were fair and kept their word. There are many groves of tamarind trees around the coast where they had their dry season camps. You can still see the remains of their stone drying kilns and the wells they dug for water, and here and there, mounds of egg-shaped stones they brought with them for ballast.

'As boys we knew who our promised wives were, if it had been arranged, but we soon learned that life was not all fun and games. From about eight or nine years of age, the uncles responsible for us began teaching us bushcraft, later supporting us at the painful circumcision and telling us not to cry out like cowards. Of course, we did not.

'As the years went by, the men led us a little bit at a time farther along the road to manhood by showing us more and more of the ceremonies. During all this time we were rigidly taught our social obligations and responsibilities. They would say things like: "You must not eat such and such a food, for that is only for proper men. Respect your parents and do as they tell you. Do not look at girls. Become a strong man so that you can look after wives and children, and do not take other men's wives."

'In the course of learning our own laws we were taken and shown the tribal boundaries, and where we could go safely and where we could not. We had much to learn.

'Nowadays we have the Christian teaching but I hope the people will not lose all the old ways and bush lore. Even though I am an ordained Christian minister, there is no mix-up in my mind because I am a tribal leader as well. I believe we can keep our ceremonies, for God gave us all things.

'Among the early missionaries to come to Goulburn Island were two Methodists, the Reverend and Mrs Watson. They were kindly people, we learned, not like the American killer who had to be executed by some of our men years before. With the setting up of a mission, our people, including my whole family, began drifting across to Goulburn Island. The missionary said he had come only to teach us about God, so girls' and boys' dormitories were set up and we were taught to read and write and to plant gardens.'

Lazarus told me many stories beside that of his life. I remember recording one which referred to north Goulburn Island and a giant who lived there, a Jun-bar-bar. I remember the fascination of Lazarus's deep voice rolling on, filling in another piece of a vast and colourful mosaic.

This is how Lazarus told the story:

'The Jun-bar-bar is a symbol of death to us, and I will tell about one who turned into a star. This Jun-bar-bar was a very big man and a boss for the Goorlie (cheeky yam) ceremony. All this was in the very beginning, in what we call Dreaming, and what you call Creation. The Goorlie ceremony was just being worked on in the Maung tribe, and was still subject to minor alterations before it could become a strict dogma like all our ceremonies.

'Jun-bar-bar decided certain things should be included, and so without consulting anyone he went away and decorated himself very beautifully with white feather down and ochre, and then sat down waiting to be summoned for this very special dance he had made. The summons was very long in coming, and finally two old men sent a messenger to tell him to await their pleasure before showing himself.

'The big man flew into a rage, stood up before all the men and shouted that he would dance then and there. "It is my law, it is my dance. You men can watch if you want to, but it will be the last time you will ever see me dance!" He strode into the clearing, stamping and singing, whirling faster and faster, his feathered form a white blur of light. Then he rose up into the sky, to shine as a star for ever in the heavens.'

The people of the East Alligator River say each night the big man once known as Jun-bar-bar stalks across the sky towards the sea and the place where Darwin now stands.

Far left:
Kundaagi in his usual form as a red kangaroo

Jun-bar-bar is closely linked to the mortuary ceremony and is supposed to take the spirits of men when they die, and this is all because, as Lazarus says, a man who wanted to dance was not allowed to.

Jun-bar-bar has become the symbol of death, and his dance is re-enacted whenever a man of the Maung tribe dies. It is also believed by this tribe that men travelling alone at night and far from their camps are in danger of Jun-bar-bar taking their spirit. A falling star is supposed to be Jun-bar-bar racing to earth to steal another man's shade. There are four cannibals in Maung mythology, and all are associated with death.

North Goulburn Island is uninhabited, but Lazarus says that once there, in early times, lived a strong hunter called Myganaich. Now Myganaich's tribe also had a Jun-bar-bar, and he lived alone at the southern end of the island and everyone kept away from him.

Early one morning Myganaich set off to cut some bark to make a dillybag and he wandered a long way looking for a suitable tree and became lost. He began searching for a way back, and failed to see the giant asleep under the shade of a clump of trees.

Flies carried the scent of Myganaich to the giant, and as soon as he sniffed the intruder he awoke, climbing to his feet angrily and demanding to know what had brought Myganaich to his preserve. Reaching for his club he bellowed, 'What you come here for? You want to fight me?'

Before Myganaich could reply the giant continued, 'I will fight you! I will fight you and then eat you all up!' He adopted a fighting stance and Myganaich could see that he would indeed have to fight or be killed where he stood. He took his own club from his belt and prepared to fight for his life. Being fleet of foot Myganaich was able at first to keep out of the giant's way, by darting in quickly and striking his own blows, then getting back out of range. Suddenly he was struck by a stray blow and fell to his knees feeling very sick. But instead of finishing him off the giant raised his club high in the air and danced around Myganaich, singing of how good a fighter he was, and how hard he could hit.

Myganaich rose groggily to his feet and the fight resumed. Somehow he managed to stay clear of the giant's blows for the next few minutes, but his strength was ebbing, and he knew that unless he could land a lucky blow and finish the giant off he would himself be crushed. Just then he realized, as though for the first time, that the giant was naked, and that if he, Myganaich, could hit his foe one vicious blow on the penis the fight would be over. So he 'set' himself and finally the chance came, and he struck with all his might and the giant fell screaming in agony, causing all the trees to shake and the land around to tremble.

When the people of the tribe heard the earth roar and shake they knew the giant was at last dead and they were glad. After resting beside his vanquished foe Myganaich returned to his people to tell them of his great victory. Naturally the people all wanted to view the body of the giant, so they followed Myganaich back to the battle scene. One old man walked to the giant's body, climbed on to the head and took out the two shining eyes.

The tribe cheered, and agreed one eye should be sent to Arnhem Land and the other to the people of the West, and this was done.

Myganaich and the giant are as real to Arnhem Land Aborigines today as they were thousands of years ago, and it is this that makes the art of Yirawala so unique; so valuable to Australia's culture.

Once, while at Goulburn Island, I witnessed the type of ceremony Yirawala paints about. Actually there were two different ceremonies, each a mortuary one. The one enacted in honour of a fine old Aborigine named Daniel will remain long in my memory. The old man had been to hospital in Darwin for an operation, and when he returned to Goulburn he was restless to see his buffalo and horses near Oenpelli on the mainland, so instead of remaining until he regained his strength, he insisted upon leaving and walking from his boat on the mainland beach. This was far too great a test for him, and he fell exhausted before he was half way, and died within minutes. When news of his death reached Goulburn Island tears swept across it like spring rains.

Traditionally, a close relative was sent to handle all the ceremonial arrangements, and a large canoe filled to capacity with other relatives came from Maningrida.

Daniel's house was smoked to cleanse it of his spirit, and all his clothing and personal possessions were burned. Close relatives were ceremoniously washed of contact with the dead man as tribal law demanded they should be. Then for several nights, and at intervals through the days, ceremonial songs were sung. Some of these songs seemed to me to be filled with urgency and to be profoundly sad.

At night the winds blew the words of the songs around Daniel's shuttered house and scattered ashes from fires he had sat beside many moons before across the camp site. I learned that those singing did so in defiance of the finality of death. As the tempo of the songs changed so did the outward mood of the singers, and they were, I was informed, conjuring

In happier times. The author holding the club of Myganaich who struck down Jun-bar-bar the giant. Next to the author on the left is Winungutj who danced the part of the giant-killer. In the centre is old Ngoloman (now deceased) father of Winungutj, and who always danced the part of the giant. On the right is Lazarus (now Rev. Lazarus Lami-Lami M.B.E.) who was the song man for the ceremony

up in their mind's eye Marlwah, the ghost symbol of the 'sugarbag' to sustain Daniel on his long journey to the spirit world. The bees are supposed to peep out from the hive at the ghost and are afraid of him. The ghost cuts open the tree, killing the bees, and as he commences eating he is sorry.

Men singers made sorry noises with their lips as they lit bunches of green leaves to smoke Daniel's house. According to mythology Daniel's ghost will also make this sorry noise in order to release all the sorrow locked in his heart as he commences his journey from the land of living people to his dreaming. Towards the end of this ceremony everyone present was called by their kin name, and the singing then broke out in another direction with both men and women joining in songs about the crows dropping out of trees to take food, the dead obviously being the food.

This ceremony was called Jambeech, and when it finished the relatives from Maningrida stepped backwards as two leaders named Ngoloman and Winoguitj led a procession of painted men and women of Goulburn Island to Daniel's house. They sang and played clapsticks and didgeridoos all the while, and thus began a phase of the Jun-bar-bar ceremony.

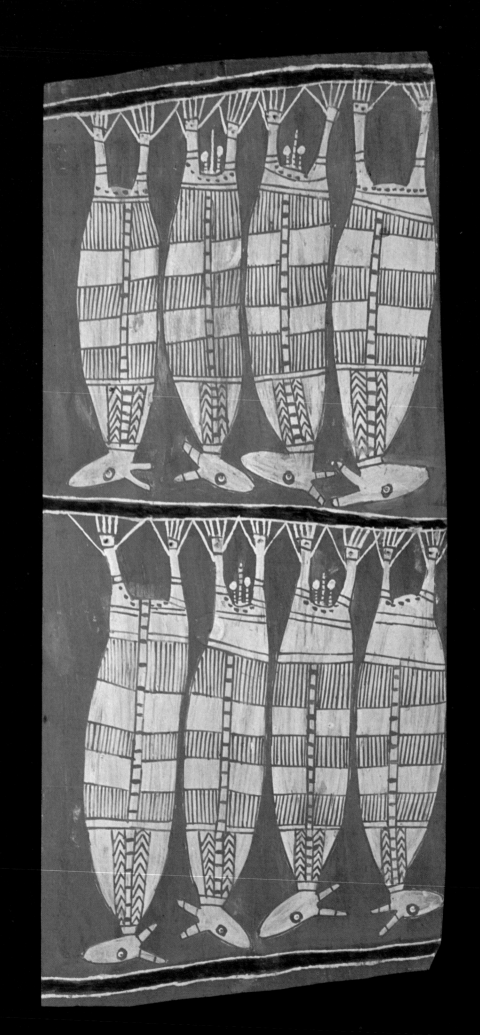

Next the men present slowly raised their right arms, faced the north, and gave an impressive salute to their imagined Islands of the Dead and to Jun-bar-bar. As the men's arms rose and fell, the motion was accompanied by three short calls, and finally by a long one which rose and fell, sighing like the outgoing tide.

At that point, Ngoloman and Winoguitj commenced leading another procession, this time comprising both men and women and a few young girls. The girls were supposed to be mermaids, and they swayed gracefully as they moved forward. Suddenly, when they reached a clearing, Ngoloman and Winoguitj divorced themselves from the rest and moved to the centre where they re-enacted the battle between Myganaich and the giant. The women took turns at singing parts of the story until close to the end, and then everyone joined in and sang in unison. It was beautifully performed, and reminded me of an opera.

The next morning the ceremony called Romm began. All the Maningrida relatives brought out the big Dinburrmija pole (associated with Barnumbirr, the Morning Star), and at the end of this ceremony the pole was presented to a young relative of the late Daniel named Solomon. While this was taking place the Maningrida men sang about the Maraian leader named Lumah-lumah who, according to mythology, was the first man to look upon the Morning Star, declared it a sacred thing, then went into the bush and cut the first Romm pole. The Morning Star, like Jun-bar-bar, is a symbol of death and because of this there is always a bunch of feathers atop the pole which are supposed to represent the eyes of the dead man and the giant.

The men began to sing now about ghosts, and I learned that when a man or woman dies, Goulburn Island Aborigines believe that the spirit goes at once to stand on top of sandhills on North Goulburn Island and to call out. Away in the unknown sea, as though in space, float the Islands of the Dead. They are three in number, and their names are Ooloorumba, Mairkon and Ningargi.

As soon as the spirit commences to call there is an old collector spirit listening to find out if the caller is male or female. If it happens to be a male, the collector scowls and paddles off to pick it up. He climbs the sandhill, seizes the ghost roughly, takes it to the canoe and orders it to paddle back to the Islands of Death. On the way the collector spirit often strikes the other with a bailing shell, or tries by other means to harm it. When they reach the Islands of Death the Jun-bar-bar rushes out and prepares to eat the new spirit. The giant is, however, usually forestalled in his intention by another spirit called Jun-bil-bil whose duty it is to drive away the Jun-bar-bar.

While the two giants fight, the older ghosts who have been watching from safety run to the new one and take it to safety. When a female ghost calls, the old collector spruces himself up to look as pleasing to the female eye as possible and sets out for her in a new bark canoe beautifully decorated with red and green parrot feathers and painted designs. When he reaches the sandhill he goes to the female ghost, gently picks it up and carries it to the canoe, settling it comfortably inside. As he paddles towards the Islands of Death he talks gently to the female spirit, and caresses it frequently.

When they land the battle between the Jun-bil-bil and Jun-bar-bar is repeated, and all the other ghosts gather around and call out to Jun-bar-bar: 'Giant, you have no friends here—go away.'

After the fight Jun-bar-bar looks about him and is sorry, because the

Far left:
Jiritja and Dua flying foxes (large fruit-eating bats) roosting. In the dance associated with this painting, men enter in line swinging bark torches from side to side. Such torches were first used by Dreaming time heroes for hunting the flying foxes. It was, in fact, a Dreaming time flying fox hero who first gave the creatures their wings, equipped with a large, curved claw on the thumb. He also invented the woomera which has a claw-like hook to anchor the spear ready for throwing

Over page:
Frilled lizards of the Ubar ceremony, with the female on the left and the male on the right. The dancers representing the lizards are painted and covered with leaves. Men armed with spears chase them and, in imitation of the animal's natural behaviour, the painted dancers climb trees and shake their backs and wave their heads from side to side. Towards the end of the Ubar ceremony, the women swing rattles made from snail shells and call out to their sons who have been with the older men who teach them about life and how to behave. When the young men have returned, the dance of the old Mimi woman begins. This is a 'cheeky' yam fertility or increase ritual to ensure a fruitful yam season. There is much more to this and to other ceremonies, but as the people regard certain parts as sacred, these are not included here

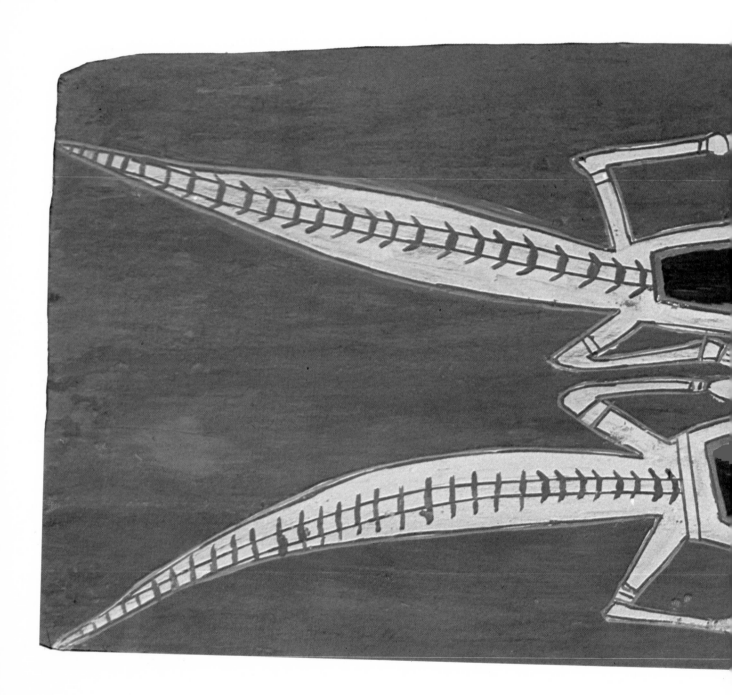

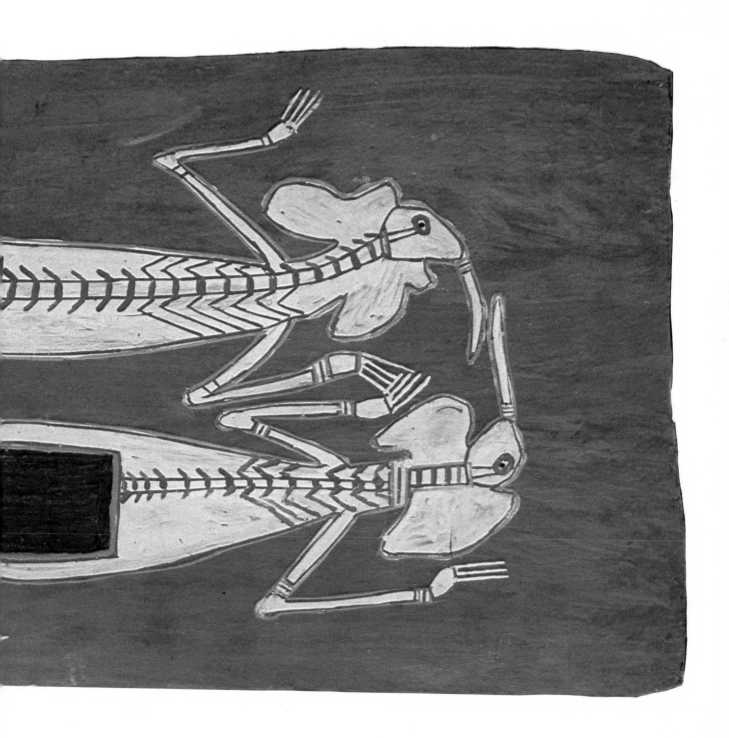

Yirrkala (Gove) men perform a sacred dance protesting against the desecration of Nhullunbuy, a sacred hill, by a mining company. The hill was the resting place of two creative ancestresses in their Dreaming time travels. Now it is crowned with a water tank for a mining community

Far right:
Paintings of the Ubar ceremony, begun by the cult heroes of the Dreaming time (Creation). Messengers (Nadjimer men) set out to invite people to the proposed Ubar ceremony (top of painting). Below them, the circle of dancers with spears play the part of Dua moiety kangaroos hopping about their tribal country, represented here by a stone and leaves at the centre of the circle. In the next scene down, owl-men paint a design on the Ubar log drum. This drum is beaten with wedge-shaped pieces of pandanus palm from the beginning of the Ubar to the end, without any break. The drumbeat is the voice of the primary creator-ancestress, variously depicted as a kangaroo-woman or a Mimi. To the left of the owl-men, a Jiritja elder paints a Dua youth in preparation
CONTINUED ON NEXT PAGE:

female ghost has gone, and he is hungry. Sometimes the good giant Jun-bil-bil loses the fight, however, and the cannibal Jun-bar-bar has his feast. When that happens the bones he leaves are always carefully collected by Jun-bil-bil who builds a skeleton which he sings to until it rises and walks into the sea where it will wait to be reborn.

Often, when a Maung mother gives birth to a weak and sickly baby she says the Jun-bar-bar ate it 'long, long time ago'. Lazarus once told me there were many Jun-bar-bar giants. He said many old people believed the Jun-bar-bar came from Indonesia in the Dreaming time. I asked Yirawala about this, and he said he thought they came from the same place as the Macassarese.

Lazarus Lami-Lami told me the story of another Jun-bar-bar and another big man. These two men, he said, lived in caves close to each other. Jun-bar-bar's diet was mainly fish which he caught each night and cleaned and shared with his wife next morning. Except for his wife, whom he was fond of, Jun-bar-bar was cruel to everybody and everything. One day a little boy wandered away from his tribal camp, crying as he went. He cried because he had no mother or father to love him, and lived with an aunt who regarded him only as a nuisance.

When the little boy became tired he sat down on some rocks to rest, but continued crying and was heard by the giant. When the giant found the little boy he scooped him into his arms and carried him back to his own camp. No one saw the giant with the little boy because as a giant he was possessed of certain magic power and was invisible. When he reached his cave the giant showed the little boy to his wife who was delighted and said the boy could work for her every day.

'He will be a good worker for me. He can get me bark every day and make me strings for my baskets, and he can make me fishing bark from the trees. He can shred it by chewing it, and he can beat it together and roll it on his thighs to make string,' she declared.

So the little boy was made to work very hard all day, every day, and

44

often his hands would bleed, and he was given very little food, and he cried more than ever now. Often, of course, he thought of running away, but he did not know the way back to his own tribe, and anyway he was afraid the giant would soon find him and bring him back. So the little boy's crying grew louder and more persistent, and worried the big man, Beet-baich-boh-booch, who went to the giant's wife and asked her what the trouble was.

She told him not to bother about it, that it was just a silly little boy crying. But Beet-baich-boh-booch was not satisfied with this explanation and demanded to see the little boy for himself.

The first thing Beet-baich-boh-booch noticed about the little boy was that his ribs were sticking out and his face was sunken. Beet-baich-boh-booch said he was going to take the little boy back to his own people, that he was starving to death. The giant's wife protested loudly, saying her husband would be furious. But the big man did not care, and he lifted the little boy on to his shoulders and strode away and shortly afterwards put the little boy down among his own people again, where he was greeted with joy by even the aunt who promised never to neglect him again.

That evening Jun-bar-bar returned to his cave, dumped his fish on the stone floor and demanded to know where the little boy was. When he learned what had happened he roared with rage, grabbed his club and rushed to the big man's cave shouting threats.

Now although Beet-baich-boh-booch was smaller than the giant he was just as strong, so he picked up his own weapon and went out to meet the challenge. The two giants made holes in the ground with their clubs, and smashed down many large trees and big rocks, and the noise of their battle was like an earthquake. Suddenly Beet-baich-boh-booch struck a deadly blow and Jun-bar-bar fell to the ground dead.

When the people learned what had happened they were happy, and all came to look upon the body of the vanquished giant.

During the visits he made to stay with me while he painted I learned that Yirawala is as much concerned with the present and future welfare of his people as he is with preserving for their culture his painting about the Dreamtime.

One day, when he appeared excessively restless, I asked him the reason. He looked at me with troubled eyes a moment, then said, 'I want take my family back to our proper land 'fore I die or go blind. I wanna stop white man from walkin' all 'bout over sacred land an' makim big holes.'

I realized Yirawala was not so much worried about the occasional white visitor who just went to the sacred places to look, as he was about the oil and mining companies which he feared would rip and tear his land apart.

He had heard from other Aborigines what had happened at Yirrkala (Gove) and at Weipa. At Weipa his people had lost large tracts of tribal land to the government and mining companies and, as Yirawala put it, were only permitted to 'sit down on little bit ground now'.

Anger gripped him, and he said, 'If we lose our dreaming we lose everything ... we like dead people then ... all finished. Plenty Aborigine say he worry 'bout law and 'bout losing land, but he not speak up. He got slack guts, just like ole woman. But me not got slack guts, me not weak. I speak up!'

During a tour of Australia I undertook with Yirawala and his paintings, which was sponsored by the Australian Council for the Arts. I learned at first hand of the thirst of people everywhere for knowledge of tribal Aborigines,

for the ceremony. To the right, two old men (termed Gandjari for this duty), sing a welcome (Nullgurrurk) to the guests as they arrive and give assurances that all will be done according to the strict, ancient tradition. At the foot of the painting are the Ubar 'cheeky' yams, so called because they are poisonous unless prepared correctly

Far left:
The artist working on a painting of Bew-bew, the giant associated with the didgeridoo

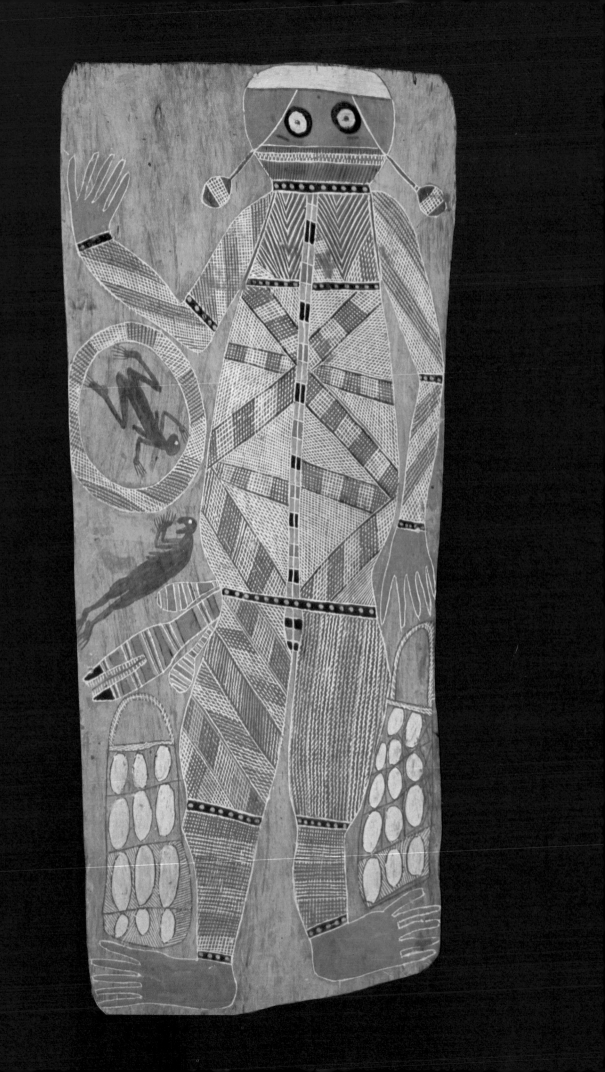

Yirawala before the bulldozers amid the smouldering remains of bushland eight kilometres from Darwin. The area yielded Aboriginal medicines, dyes and pigments. It was also the habitat of the red-tailed black cockatoo

Far left:
Bew-bew returning home with some goose eggs for the two girls he held prisoner

and for explanations of their mythology. Perhaps I should not have been surprised at this. I am still learning about it myself; still fascinated by its beauty and depth of feeling.

Here is another story Yirawala painted about and related to me:

Out on the mud flats at the northern end of Goulburn Island there once lived a giant named Bew-bew, and his house was made of mud and sticks, and was cone-shaped. The name of the house was Boonji, which means 'blind'. It was called that because it had no door and entry was gained through a hole at the top of the cone; the occupants of houses like this lowered themselves on to the floor by a string ladder called an *arrowk*. The

Yirawala gathering white clay at the Dripstone Caves. The clay will be used as the base for white paint. It is very powdery and free of grit. The Caves area yields clay of several different colours

house was built like this as protection against mosquitoes.

Bew-bew lived on freshwater things such as goose eggs and lily-roots, tortoise and fish. One morning Bew-bew was preparing to go hunting when he saw two young girls coming towards his house, they were lost and had reached his house accidentally. When Bew-bew saw them he smiled broadly and said, 'Welcome, my two wives.'

He picked up the two girls and dropped them down the cone of his house, pulling up the ladder afterwards so they could not escape. When Bew-bew came home that evening he fed the girls and was happy that he had found two such lovely young wives. But the girls were terrified of him,

48

and pleaded with him to leave them alone. But not being a good giant Bew-bew could not do that. The elder girl was more afraid for her sister than for herself, as the younger one was very young, and small. The girls did not want Bew-bew as a husband, and before going to sleep again asked him to leave them alone.

Bew-bew smiled but said nothing. But during the night he took them both to his body by force.

Next morning the girls were very sick and could not walk. Bew-bew went out hunting and brought home waterlily roots and fish, but the girls were too sick to eat. Bew-bew being dull-witted thought they had not eaten because the food did not please them, so he brought home goose eggs the next morning. Later he went away again, and when he had not returned by mid-morning the girls decided to escape, and the elder one stood on the shoulders of the younger one and pulled herself through the hole at the top of the cone and then turned around, bent down, and grasped the hands of her sister and pulled her to safety.

As the younger girl could still not walk her sister carried her on her shoulders back to the camp of their people. When they arrived their own people ran to them, asking what had happened and why the younger one could not walk. When they learned what had happened they were very angry at Bew-bew, and they cried for the girls and the dreadful thing that had happened to them.

Later that day Bew-bew returned to his house with two dilly-bags full of goose eggs for his two wives. When he discovered they had escaped he threw the bags on the ground and bellowed with rage. Snatching up his club, which was as large as a tree trunk, he rushed off to find the girls, smashing down trees as he went. Now the people of the girls' camp heard this noise and knew he would kill them all unless they did something to prevent him. So they worked hard and dug a huge pit on the path to their camp which they covered with saplings and branches and dirt until it looked just like ordinary ground.

Soon they saw the giant Bew-bew coming, shouting and knocking down trees, and kicking huge rocks from his path, and he was shouting, 'I'll kill you . . . I'll kill you all and take back my two wives.'

When Bew-bew reached a spot near the pit he stopped and looked about him in surprise, wondering where all the people had gone. He commenced stamping wildly about, still shouting with anger, then he stood on the trap and fell into the pit.

All the people ran from the bush where they had been hiding and attacked Bew-bew until his great body was like a porcupine, with so many spears sticking out of it. Quickly now the people started to push dirt on to Bew-bew, and in a spasm of pain the giant reached down and put his penis into his mouth and commenced blowing on it. The noise which came from it made a 'didgenbraw, didgenbraw, didgenbraw' sound. The men above stopped pushing in the dirt and leaned forward the better to hear the sound, which they decided they liked.

They decided to try it themselves, but discovered that no normal man could achieve it, so they went off into the bush looking for something to use as a substitute. They chopped down a number of trees until at last they found one with a hollow trunk which, when blown, made a similar noise to Bew-bew's penis.

And so, on Goulburn Island today, the people say that a man who can play the didgeridoo well plays like Bew-bew . . . .

The concern Yirawala had earlier expressed to me about the future of his people and for the preservation of tribal lands was brought home to me with force one day when I was taking him to Dripstone Caves, a few miles from Darwin. He had asked to go there to collect ochre which he uses as paint, and to cut some bark for his painting on the way.

As we neared the caves I was surprised to see dust rising in a heavy cloud from beyond a hill, and smoke smudging the skyline in another direction. As we topped the crest of the road both Yirawala and I were shocked to see great heaps of trees had been torn from the ground, as though some mythological giant had been on a rampage, and huge hollows of land gaping. All the trees were burning, and several bulldozers were chewing into the earth while overhead a flock of red-tailed black cockatoos were circling, and crying out as though in protest at their haven being destroyed.

As I brought the vehicle to a stop Yirawala leapt from it shouting, 'What they do? . . . spoilim all th' bush . . . all my special place . . . spoil wallabies an' birds. Look! Poor damn cockatoo . . . him got no home now. . . .'

Before I could stop him the old man ran across the disfigured land and took up a defiant stance in front of one of the bulldozers. His cries of protest were drowned out by the roar of the machine, and I feared he might be run down. When within a few feet of Yirawala, the bulldozer driver brought his machine to a grinding halt, looked at me and shouted, 'Get this silly old bastard out of here!'

I took my old friend by the left arm and led him away gently. I was disturbed by the look in his eyes which were filled with tears. He was like a man in a dream. His lower lips shook, and he muttered, 'They spoil it all . . . they do very bad thing. . . .'

At Dripstone Caves I encouraged Yirawala to rest in the cool shade awhile, and soon he was puffing on his pipe, but the sadness was still in his eyes, and he said, 'White people spoil it all . . . we can't stay here . . . where to go? What we do? . . .'

'I'm sorry, Yirawala,' was all I could find to say, and at that moment I was painfully conscious of the difference in our colour, and my white flesh did not fill me with pride.

Soon the old painter began talking freely, and it was all about the tribal Aborigines' ties with the land and of how the white man had moved into it and established large cattle stations and built mines.

'We people no own any more land. Got no paper in hand to prove it, only cave drawing in my country. Orright, we people work hard on stations, plenty good work, too. But only get little bit money . . . an' now there plenty white man come to take stockman job away from my people an' wives an' children get kicked out to starve . . . where we go, I ask? What we do?' Yirawala asked.

That evening, after dinner, Yirawala seated himself in the lounge and said, 'We make big talk now.' He talked for almost three hours. The theme of it was his fear for the welfare of his own tribe, the Gunwinggus, whose tribal land takes in the Oenpelli area of Arnhem Land.

He had heard that a mining company had commenced operations near Oenpelli, and he was afraid the tribal sacred places were in danger. In particular he was afraid his own family caves which were on the edge of the escarpment country, where the Liverpool River dissolves into many waterholes, were threatened.

He wanted me to get Landrovers and take his family to see the place where their bloodlines commenced to flow. 'Lovely country that. Plenty fish . . . plenty kangaroo . . . plenty bird, too. An' lotta drawings, too, from my father an' grandfather from, oh, long, long time 'go.

'I want you an' ole man take pictures—keepim for me an' family . . . we don't want lose that dreaming an' law. You makim picture an' keepim.' He pointed to his eyes and said, 'I got no good eyes now . . . might be blind pretty soon. You take me see caves pretty quick. What you reckon?'

I knew there would be considerable difficulty doing what my friend asked, and I realized explaining the problems to him would prove hard, so I told him I would give the matter some thought before answering one way or the other.

I knew that the Aborigines were losing their land and their identity, and that his eyes were failing; that if he did not see his caves soon he might never see them. An eye specialist had told me only a prompt operation could preserve his sight. But Yirawala did not have confidence and would not agree. 'I can see orright, little bit,' he said.

Finally I sent Yirawala for a holiday to Melville Island with his son while I went quietly off to Sydney to seek financial backing to take Yirawala and his family to his caves. In Sydney I spoke first to Professor Elkin who already knew of my friends, and knows the Gunwinggu people well, being a world authority on the Australian Aborigines.

Professor Elkin suggested I should approach some of the big business houses and promise to give credit to them publicly for any help they provided. He explained he had been successful in this way when seeking funds to film documentaries about tribal Aborigines.

This sounded a good idea, and I tried it, but I had no luck. Although many executives expressed interest, none offered money. I was almost at the end of my tether when I went to television producer Robert Raymond and asked if he could offer any suggestions. He said he could, and he approached Channel Seven with the result that between the television station and the National Museum $10,000 was made available to me to take a full photographic crew and Yirawala's family into Arnhem Land and the cave country. We were obliged also to take along a white Welfare officer from Darwin.

However, before we finally got away from Darwin I encountered a number of objections to my plans from Northern Territory Administration officials. In fact, at one stage it seemed as though we would be frustrated in our well-laid plans; that the Wet season would engulf the country before we were on our way. At this point Yirawala wrote a moving plea to Mr Harry Giese, Director of Aboriginal Affairs, explaining that if he were not allowed to go then he feared he would never see his caves.

Still Mr Giese did not relent.

Finally the intervention of the *Darwin News*, backed by support for us from Mr Ron Withnall, a member of the Northern Territory Legislative Council, encouraged the director to relent, and we were eventually given permission. There were three Landrovers and eight in our party which included Oscar Scherl, our cameraman, my husband Cecil, the film director, mechanics and drivers and myself handling sound and continuity.

When we reached the first of Yirawala's caves the old man ran to an outcrop of rock, climbed it, then raised his arms high above his head, closed his eyes as if communicating with someone or something distant and then gave a series of long, strange calls.

Later he confided to me that he had been advising the ghosts of his ancestors that he had come home. I felt that day closer to the Aboriginal

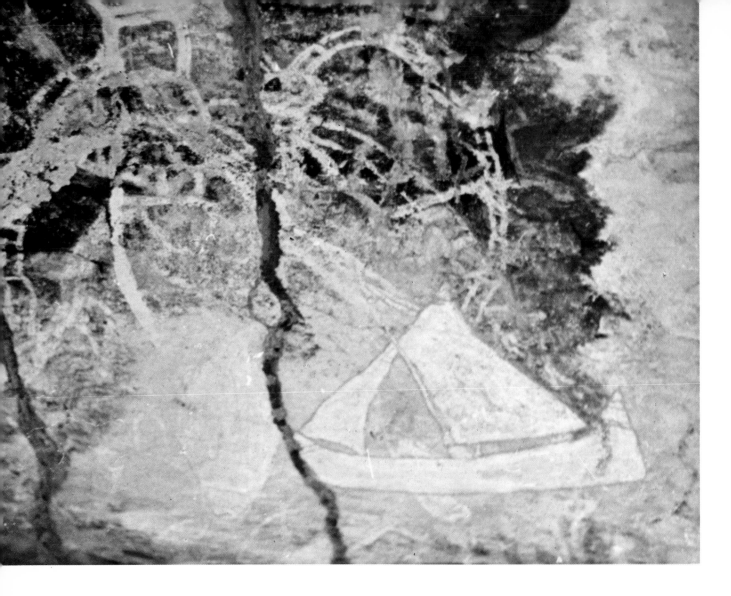

Old paintings in Yirawala's family caves. The sailing craft is most likely a Macassarese prau

mythology than ever before. Perhaps the beautiful country with its valleys and rolling hills and rocks like great marbles stretching for as far as I could see generated some sort of spiritual sense within me. I don't know.
But I do know that if scenery can be awe-inspiring this country was of that type. It was filled with peace, beauty and mystery.

Yirawala took great pleasure in pointing out to us places he remembered from the stories his grandfather had told him about the cave area.
There were long holes, as smooth as silk, going all the way through huge rocks, and in one rock face we saw what appeared to be circular fossilized shells protruding, which looked like ammonites I had seen elsewhere.
Yirawala said his grandfather had told him that once great waters had been here.

On a jutting outcrop of rock we found some drawings of many fish and one particular fish appeared to be attacking a woman. Yirawala said that this old man had turned himself into a giant fish and had eaten his unfaithful wife when she went into the water.

On another rock face we found a drawing of a giant with a very large penis and nearby two women. Yirawala was telling his sons, Danny and Bobby, the story about it in his native tongue, and every now and then the three would laugh, and glance at the rest of us shyly. I heard him say the name 'Bew-bew', and asked him if this was a drawing of the giant who had

raped the two sisters in the mythology, and he agreed it was.

Other drawings depicted Kundaagi, the kangaroo man, killing his wife with a spear because of her unfaithfulness. These figures were human bodies with kangaroo heads. Here and there were drawings of the Mimi people, a mythological race of small people with very long, thin necks who were supposed to have been responsible for some of the cave wall and ceiling paintings and drawings in Arnhem Land. Most were shown in aggressive poses except one—a large black figure of Mother Earth, with her arms by her side.

In the rock clefts there were remains of Lorrgon logs with bones protruding, and with skulls and bones which had obviously been disturbed centuries ago by wild animals. There were also small, cave-like 'gutters' and what appeared to have once been entrances filled with the heavy bones of a human being who had apparently been eaten.

Yirawala explained that apart from ritual cannibal acts, people long ago would sometimes eat a young person who strayed from his own tribe. He showed me how this happened by using mime.

He said: 'Young boy walkabout here an' men of tribe say, "you look 'ere".' Pointing dramatically Yirawala pretended to be indicating a goanna, then he continued; ' "Big goanna in there . . . you crawl in catchim. Good tucker that one".'

Human skeletal fragments in a cave in Yirawala's country

53

He went through the motions of several men encouraging the boy, then changed roles to become the boy anxiously looking into a small cave, then crawling quickly inside. Next Yirawala was playing the role of the men again, filling up the mouth of the cave with rocks and small stones, dry wood and grass. He looked up to make sure I was following him, then he said, 'Now lit fire. Pretty quick boy cook. Then men wait for rocks to cool before taking out boy to eat.'

When Yirawala began showing signs of weariness we called a halt to the filming and explorations for the day, but I continued looking around for a little while longer near our camp and found a large tunnel inside of which I discovered countless bats which squeaked around my head. Outside the tunnel there was a big shrub with green berries, and later I learned that Aborigines often used these berries for catching fish by crushing them into fluid and then pouring it into the lagoon. Apparently it had an intoxicating effect upon the fish which did not in any way degrade their taste or food value.

The following morning we had been away from camp only a short while when I saw a cave about twelve metres up a rock face. We went to investigate it and on the ceiling was a painting that looked like half man, half crocodile. Yirawala's explanation was that this was like evil magic, a type of sorcery painting. Yirawala said the monster had once been a man named 'Geechnoch' who had been driven from his tribe because he was a social misfit, and always causing trouble.

Being a magician he turned himself into a being that was half crocodile, half man, and lived in a rock hole just below the waterline of a lagoon. His main diet was men. 'See long claws on feet an' hand? Him bad magic feller,' Yirawala said seriously.

Later that day we came to a cave with a large flat stone in the centre. Oscar Schirl said it reminded him of an altar so we called it 'Altar Rock'. The surface of the rock was smooth and dotted with round, smooth holes. In the sand around the rock were the remains of old fires and half buried in ashes were painted bones of small kangaroos, some yellow with age. Yirawala said the bones were the result of many ceremonies held to celebrate a young warrior's first kill of a kangaroo.

On the surface of the rock were a number of stone spearheads, scrapers, knives, and a few axe heads. Near the rear of the cave there was a narrow cleft and I could see a number of bones and a small skull. I was told this was where a woman ate parts of a dead baby she had borne to get back its spirit. Usually such babies had died from natural causes or as the result of an accident.

About this time I commenced having trouble with the welfare officer. This generally was because he would insist upon us going in one direction while Yirawala would want to go in another. As the expedition was inspired by Yirawala in the first place I believed he should have the final say in this; it was his country, and he knew what he wanted us to film.

Once, after the welfare officer had threatened to revoke our permits to travel in native land unless we were prepared to do as he said, Yirawala trembled with emotion, and said, 'Me big boss for this country. Welfare man no know damn thing 'bout place . . . this properly my country, me number one boss. Only I say where we go. An' I do nothing wrong.'

Eventually we worked out an uneasy truce, and the welfare officer reluctantly agreed to let Yirawala plot some of our course. He took us into rich, green, heavy bush country where we camped night by night for

Far right:
Geechnoch, the lazy misfit, catching a fish. Driven from his tribe for trouble-making, he turned himself into a creature— half man, half crocodile—that feeds on men who come to his waterhole

54

several days. The going was hard here, but it was worth the effort; there was a tremendous variety of wildlife, with big owls, parrots and, occasionally, a kangaroo would come into sight.

On the third day we stopped beside a creek with a deep pool at one end of it. The water was mirror clear, reflecting the bright green Pandanus palms surrounding it on three sides. Yirawala refused us permission to film here. He explained it was a sacred place, and the Yowk-yowk water women would not like it. He also warned us against breaking any tree branches or pulling any grass.

'Pullem grass might makim water women angry . . . then big storm an' flood come. Better not touch,' Yirawala said.

He went on to tell me that the water women were light skinned because they lived deep in the spring of the pool, only surfacing to sing and dance and make ceremonies. They are, he said, beautiful, with long black hair and smooth skin.

Yirawala then told me the story of the Dreaming Man who was very clever. He captured one of the water women and took her to his camp for a wife. The woman had pointed, sharp teeth which he had not seen before, so the Dreaming Man put a stone in her mouth so she could not bite him and tied her hands. Back at his camp he put her in a heavy smoke fire, sang songs to her and made magic to make her forget the sound of water and her longing to be back in the pool.

The Dreaming Man's uncle told him never to allow the woman to go to fetch water, as she would dive into the pool and never return. Well, the couple lived happily enough until the Dreaming Man forgot his uncle's warning and sent the lovely, ageless woman for water, and he never saw her again, and he was left very sad and alone.

At the end of one month's travelling, filming, and listening to Yirawala's seemingly bottomless well of stories the Wet commenced to come in, and we returned to Darwin as fast as we could. The first few days back in civilization were spent tidying up our material. After that was done Yirawala left for Croker Island and I flew down to Sydney with my husband to see the 'rushes' of the film.

I watched this in the company of Robert Raymond and Professor Elkin. It seemed a fine film, Yirawala and his family were superb, and I knew that with the appropriate music and sounds dubbed in it would prove a valuable contribution to the study of the tribal Aborigines.

Shortly after viewing the film I sent word to Yirawala that because it had been so well received I would probably obtain a grant from the Australian Council for the Arts, and take him and his paintings for display and lectures throughout the southern states, and that this would more than likely be our next adventure together.

This was, I believed, the only thing left I must try to do before the old man, the finest of all Aboriginal traditional painters, walked away into the wild country to quietly await his Dreaming and his meeting with his ancestors.

At this time I did not even guess that the Member of the British Empire would be bestowed upon him. I was pleased he was honoured in this way. He richly deserved it.

Now, when he goes to his Dreaming he will be remembered always, and his art will live on to remind us of the wealth of meaning behind it, and we can all be the richer for studying it and learning something of the culture of our dark-skinned brothers and sisters.

The death of Lumah-lumah
Far right:
The vengeful mainland tribesmen set out to Goireeba. The dark men in the top canoe belong to the Dua moiety, the pale men below to the Jiritja moiety. The men chant and work up their anger for the coming battle
Over page:
Before dying, Lumah-lumah cuts himself in the rarrk pattern and sings a new ceremony to the tribes—the beginnings of the Maraian. Lumah-lumah first saw and named the Morning Star, the white fish, and other animals and objects associated with the Maraian ceremony of today

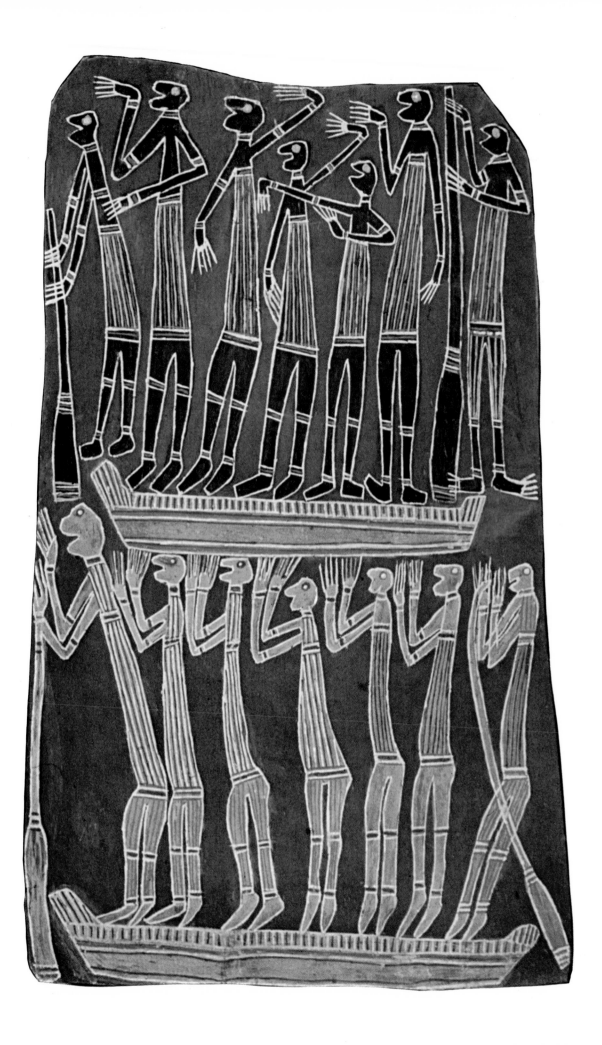

LUMAH-LUMAH, THE BIG MARAIAN MAN

This is Yirawala's impression of Lumah-lumah. He was a giant or monster washed up from the Maccassen Island during a furious storm, and came to rest on the small island of Goireeba, in the Crocodile Islands group. He remained there until he died.

Lumah-lumah had two very attractive young daughters, and they spent most of their time collecting shellfish on the beaches. The people on the mainland opposite Goireeba used to hear strange noises coming from the islands. They thought it sounded like a great conch shell which blew every now and then.

After a while their curiosity got the better of them and they sent three men out in a canoe to investigate. The men took food and water for a long journey, and weapons and fishing lines and a turtle spear and rope.

In the late afternoon their bark canoe grounded on sand at a little island and the men stepped out, looking around nervously and wondering what was going to happen. Soon two pretty young girls approached and said the

The death of Lumah-lumah
The battle in progress. Axes and spears of the mainland tribesmen rain down on the giant

59

Explanations of Maraian designs

(1) Represents a sacred water-hole, the life-source for Gunwinggu country. This design is painted on a young man going through his third Maraian ceremony. Each time the ceremony is performed the young man is taken one stage further towards full knowledge of the ancient and sacred mysteries. This progressive revelation takes many years (Jiritja moiety)

(2) A Mimi from the beginnings of the Maraian. According to tradition, the Mimi people were very early inhabitants of the land. When they died they turned into spirits whose duties include guarding sacred caves and ensuring the natural increase of kangaroos and yams. Mimis began many ceremonies still performed to this day (Jiritja moiety)

(3) The same Mimi man as in (2). He is removing his limbs before taking the form of a fish to enter a life-source waterhole in the Gunwinggu country. Today, the symbols of ancestors, the painted wooden ranga, are kept in sacred waterholes. These ancestral spirits began the ceremonies, and are called upon when needed to sanction them. This dependence on the ancestral spirits emphasizes the importance of stability and continuity in Aboriginal traditional life. This Mimi carries his child around his neck. In the old days, only men could carry the children of important leaders. (Jiritja moiety)

(4) Designs for painting on men in the Maraian. They represent the seasons, the Wet and the Dry. (Jiritja moiety)

(5) These criss-cross patterns or rarrk were first devised by the giant Lumah-lumah. Rarrk is used to decorate older men taking part in a Maraian. (Jiritja moiety)
CONTINUED ON NEXT PAGE:

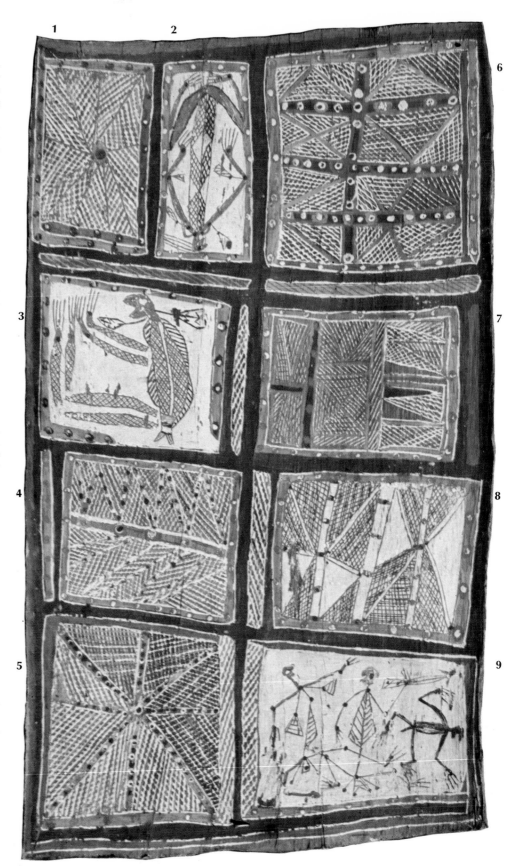

(6) This design is associated with Jinaroo, the spirit of the wind that brings the Wet. It represents clouds, rain, and the 'power' stones used for calling down rain and storm. Like the rarrk, this design is used in painting men for the Maraian. (Dua moiety)

(7) Another design associated with wind and storm. The triangular sections represent storm centres over Gunwinggu country. It is used on fully initiated old men in the Maraian. (Dua moiety)

(8) Clear skies and white clouds following a storm. Again used in painting older men. (Dua moiety)

(9) Small black figure is the ancient Mimi who first taught the Maraian. (Dua moiety)

Note: None of the information here, or anywhere in the book, is of a 'Jeep' or secret nature, so as to avoid sacrilegious exposure of certain parts of traditional Aboriginal life and belief

Lumah-lumah, the primary figure of the Maraian ceremony. This giant was brought from somewhere near Indonesia by a cyclone which flung him into a coastal islet called Goireeba long, long ago. Yirawala presents Lumah-lumah singing parts of the Maraian which he composed. The story of Lumah-lumah is told by other tribes besides the Gunwinggu. Maraian is used for anything sacred and powerful, in place of words that are sacrosanct and thus known only to the older, fully-initiated men

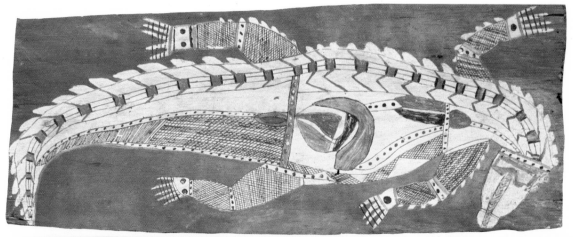

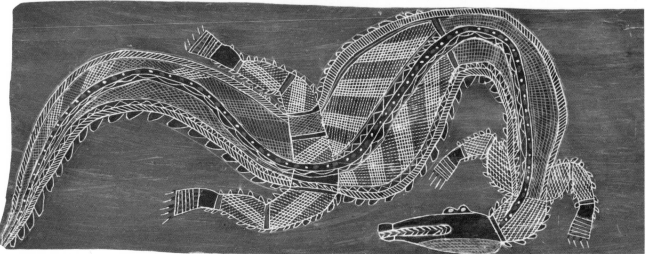

*Maraian crocodiles
Above:
The whiter crocodile's 'organs'
are actually sacred stones
Below:
This represents the spirit of the
crocodile dancing on ceremonial
grounds*

*Lumah-lumah was the first to see
and name the crocodile*

men could spend the night with them. The men eagerly agreed to this, and during the night used the girls in turn. However, before sleep overtook them they began to feel uneasy, and feared their apparent good fortune might in reality be a trap, so they held a whispered consultation and agreed that they should creep away from the girls and go to their canoe.
They did this, reaching the canoe just as dawn was breaking.

The jumped into their craft and began paddling for all they were worth, but before they had gone a kilometre their canoe began to disobey their efforts, and drifted back to the island.

The noise of trees crashing reached their ears and a huge man stepped from the bush on to the beach and cursed them for having come to his island. Fire blasted from the huge man's mouth as he spoke. 'You are going to die!' he shouted, adding, 'but first I will eat your canoe and everything in it,' and he began crunching up the canoe, and then the turtle spear and rope, the paddles and the weapons.

After this he turned to the men and said, 'Let me swallow you now.'

62

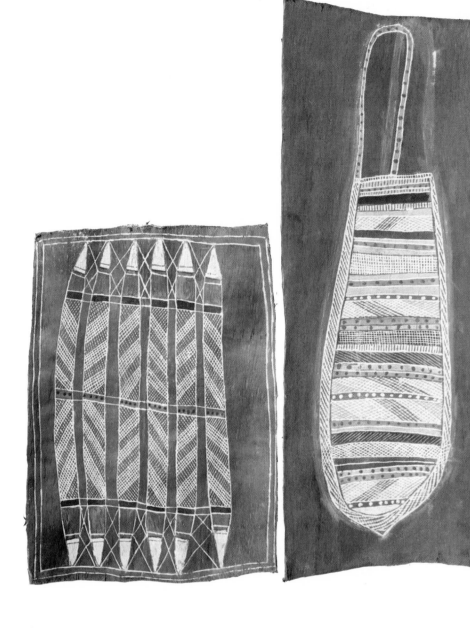

Yams and dillybag—Maraian. The dillybag (Walarnaar) is made to give to children of seven or eight years as a sort of reminder of their birth and early childhood. It may also be a gift between adult friends or lovers, as a sign of esteem or affection. The dillybag is made of pandanus palm strips, gaily painted, and sometimes incorporating part of the child's umbilical cord

The yams are done in the old style of body painting, in which the yams are shown growing and spreading. In the Dreaming time yams moved about above ground like men

The men could not move as the monster picked them up and ate them.

Lumah-lumah went back to his camp to sleep, but he could not do so as indigestion bothered him and caused him to make wind—a 'big noise sounding like a conch shell.' The people on the mainland heard this noise and wondered what it was. They were concerned that the three men had not returned, and after a few more days sent another expedition to find out what had happened. This time it was two canoes and six men. These men, too, arrived at the island and were met by the girls who fed them and let the men use them as their wives.

In the middle of the night these men also began to feel afraid and crept

63

Left:
Maraian ceremonial stick used by the Gunwinggu. The designs represent sacred waterholes, rain and clouds, and the sacred rarrk pattern first introduced by Lumah-lumah

Right:
Wurlurr the white rock wallaby feeding on wild fruits and berries. There is a dance in the Maraian concerning Wurlurr

64

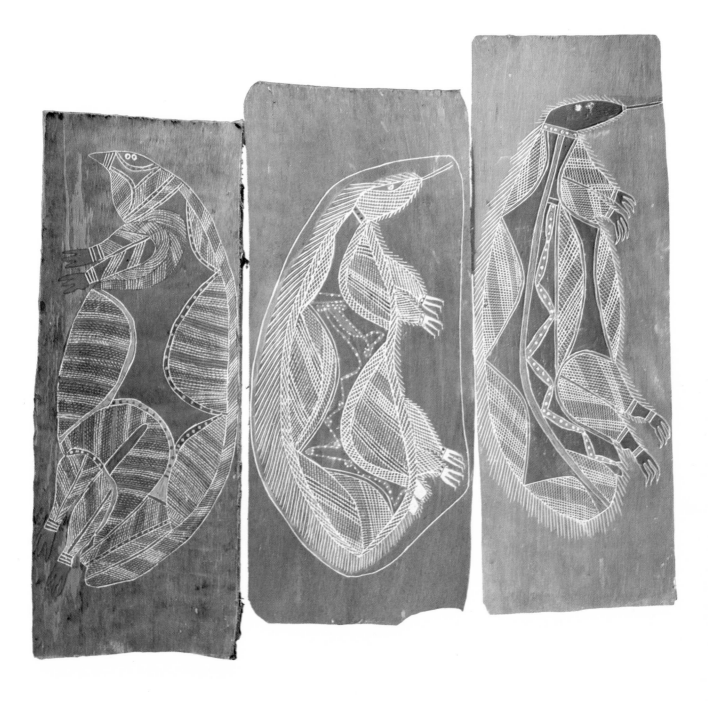

away from the sleeping girls. They too paddled about a kilometre and experienced the drift backwards of their craft, because Lumah-lumah had magic over the seas. When the two canoes touched the shore the monster rushed out as before and the people on the mainland heard again the loud noises and lit smoke fires as a signal to the men to return.

They waited some days, and when the men failed to return they talked of making war.

Anteaters, Maraian ceremony

The line around the middle one indicates that it is underground.
(See caption on Nutmungi p. 66)

Bonefish (above) *and white fish* (below). *Each is associated with an important dance. Four men dance the bonefish dance at the start of the Maraian, then ten men dance the white fish dance*

Far right above: *The barramundi—another dance in the Maraian*

Far right below: *Nutmungi. In the Dreaming time Nutmungi walked about as a man, as did the spiny anteater. The two fought over a woman. The anteater hurled rocks at Nutmungi. So badly bruised was he that he fell into a waterhole and could not stand up again. To this day the tortoise inhabits waterholes and crawls about with the lumps and marks on his back from the rocks hurled by the anteater. During this fight, Nutmungi threw so many spears at the anteater that he also was forced to crawl away, the spears becoming spines. Ten men dance this third dance of the Maraian*

A spear was driven into the ground and white ochre thrown. Messages were sent to Rowland Bay, Johnson Bay, Maningrida, Cape Stuart and Blythe Bay, summoning the people to Cape Stuart to fight.

Many canoes arrived and about five hundred men set off in the early morning, painted with white ochre. As the canoes neared the island of Goireeba the men sang and worked themselves into a rage, waving their weapons and shouting threats. At a given signal each man lit up his bark torch (irraich) and they ringed the island and gradually commenced moving into the centre in an ever-tightening circle.

The men threw their torches into the dry bush and flames were soon roaring ahead of them, towards the camp of the giant. He awoke from sleep and jumped up, half blinded by smoke and flames. The men saw him half burned and rushed forward, hurling spears, clubs and axes. Soon Lumah-lumah was on his knees with hundreds of spears quivering in his back and the earth around him red with his blood. Beneath him were the bodies of many mainland men, all badly mangled.

Before the remaining men could finish Lumah-lumah off he rose to his knees, lifted his arms and said, 'Do not kill me. I will teach you new law.'

He picked up two large clapsticks, beat them together and sang a sacred song. (And this song is still sung today.)

Then he picked up sharp flint stones and cut criss-cross designs upon his body, and this is the pattern used in all Maraian paintings today.

It is called 'rarrk.'

When all the cuts had been made the giant instructed the people to cut up his body and take his bones to the mainland, but his huge size made this

66

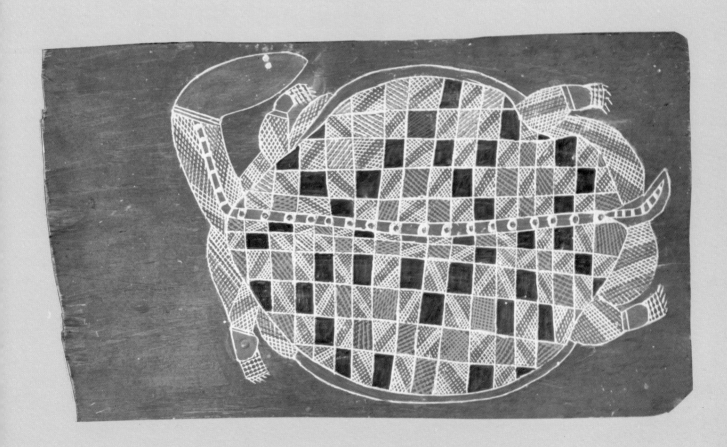

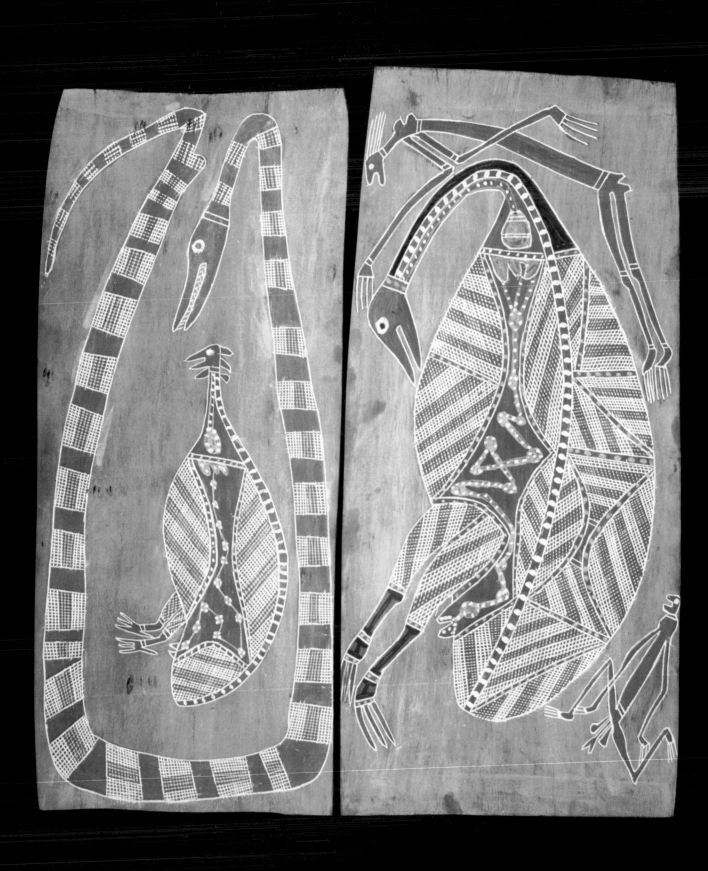

Kundaagi, the red plains kangaroo, being speared by Mimis. After taking his body fat, they pulled his skin back over his bones and brought him back to life. When a hunter kills a thin kangaroo, he can always say that the Mimis got to it before him. (Sixth dance in the Maraian)

Far left:
Daadbi the poison snake and Birrap-birrap the little bird. Four men do the Daadbi dance, followed by two doing the Birrap-birrap dance. (Fourth and fifth in the Maraian)

Far right:
Turkey pursued by Mimis for his body fat. The turkey finally said, 'I am a man like you, leave me alone', and at this, turned into a man. (Maraian)

impossible, so the people compromised. They took sections of the bones and the vital organs. Dua took the heart, lungs, kidneys and all round bones. Jiritja took all the long bones and long organs. In the Maraian ceremony, painted designs and symbols of wood and stone represent those bones and organs of Lumah-lumah.

Four men dance the bone fish dance (Jiritja)
Ten men dance the white fish dance (Jiritja)
Ten men dance the freshwater turtle dance (Jiritja)
Four men dance the Daadbi dance (Dua)
Two men dance Barrap-barrap, the small white seabird with feathers of red on its head (Dua)

(Interval)

Dance of Kundaagi, the red plains kangaroo (Jiritja)
Dance of the turkey (Dua).

Far left:
Turkey eating bush fruits. The turkey dance is the seventh dance in Maraian, and is restricted totally to fully initiated men
Far right:
Stork eating fish. The stork or Jabiru (Xenorhynchus asiaticus) represents still another Maraian dance and song

Maraian whitefish design, as painted on the bodies of the older men of high ceremonial status for the Maraian.

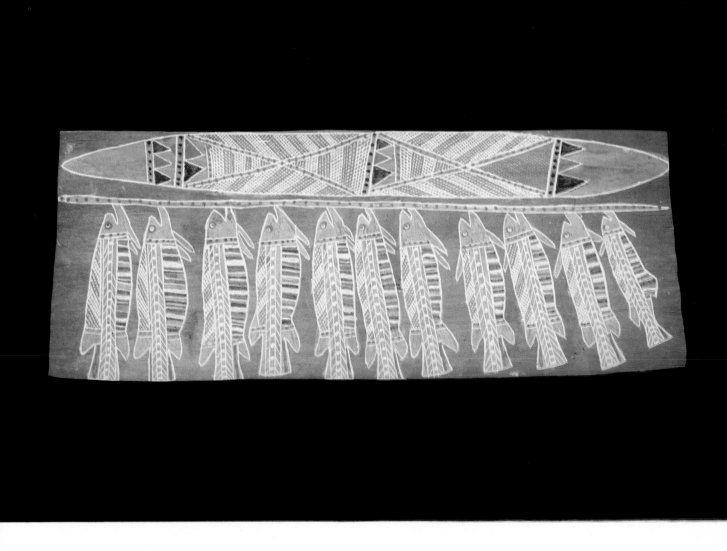

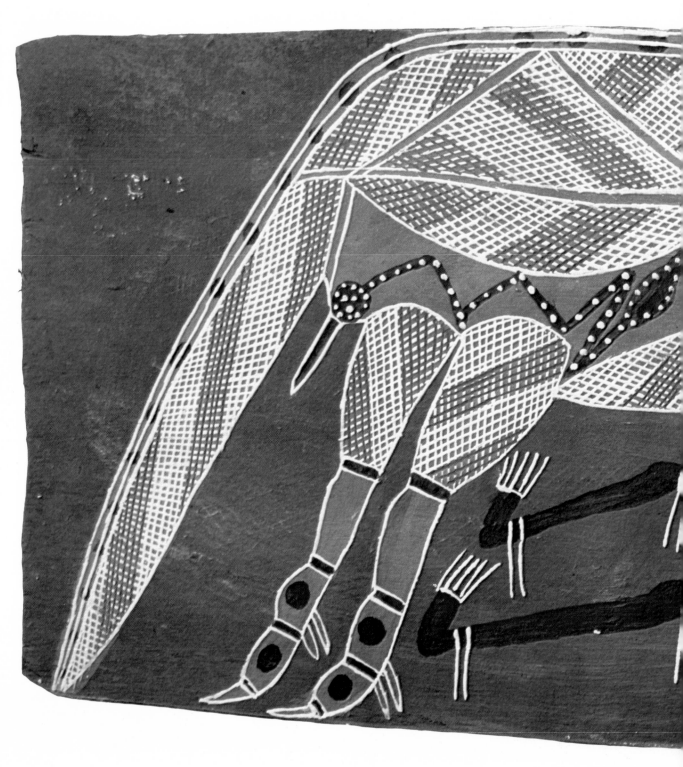

Kundaagi speared to death by one of the Mimis

Namarrgine. His evil magic earned him punishment from the tribe. After death his spirit could become visible as a swamp bird. Now he steals the spirits of children

74

NAMARRGINE, THE BIRDMAN

Yirawala showed me a painting he had completed at my home one day and told me it represented a story about an evil man who practised black medicine and ate human flesh. Many people, he said, died because of this man's evil. This is the story he related:

Because of his evil influence, Namarrgine was driven off by all the other people, and he went to live in a cave by himself. When he died he took the form of a swamp bird that walks around all night calling 'kowk-kowk-kowk.'

Whenever a child is crying and cannot sleep the mother may whisper to it: 'Look out! Namarrgine is walking . . . you go to sleep now and don't make a noise.'

Namarrgine is invisible, but he can take the form of a visible swamp bird. If a child is sick and growing thinner and his or her skin is turning to a blackish-grey colour people will say that it must die because Namarrgine has already taken the spirit from the body.

This painting shows the evil magician stealing the soul of a sick child. Namarrgine has long fingernails which he can extend to any length, and these crawl over the ground like snakes to fasten on to the soul of the sick child and draw it out.

I asked Yirawala whether he had actually heard of a case which proved people really did believe in the evil of Namarrgine, and he said he did. He then told me of some relations of his who had a sick baby when living near the Oenpelli Mission.

These people lived on a cattle station some miles from the mission, and when their baby became ill and they could not obtain proper help at the homestead they decided to walk to Oenpelli Mission in the hope that the 'doctor plane' would come and help them.

According to Yirawala his relatives trudged along the dusty bush track in the fierce heat. The woman's face was set in grim lines of fear, and the baby was held closely to her, and she talked gently to it all the time. She was desperate, and she was unable to understand why the station Missus' had been not more interested in her baby than to offer a few aspros.
The Mission was the place for help, so she and her husband must get there, was her reasoning. . . .

As the two parents walked on, pushing through long, dry grass, kites circled overhead, hawking their tune of death.

Finally the father ran ahead, hoping to see signs of habitation which would offer assistance, but he found nothing and returned to his wife. He urged her to hurry, saying that if they could only reach Red Lily Lagoon they could refresh themselves, cool the baby's hot skin and then carry on.

But before they reached the fringe of the lagoon a white cockatoo, the symbol of death, flew overhead and the woman glanced fearfully at her baby. The husband told his wife to rest while he ran ahead to fetch water for her and the child, and when he returned the woman tried to 'feed' a few drops of the cool water into the baby's mouth, but there was no movement, and the closed eyes did not open.

The mother pulled aside the ragged blanket used as a shawl and placed her head near the child's protruding ribs. As she did so the tiny heart fluttered, then ceased to beat. The mother's face twisted into a picture of agony, and she cried out once, loudly.

And the people who later learned what had happened whispered that the baby had been taken by Namarrgine.

'Namarrgine has taken another soul from a baby,' they said, and were afraid. . . .

Two Dreaming time kangaroo-people copulating. The scene painted here is part of an extremely old legend. A woman once refused her husband's attentions, claiming that he was too old and repulsive. Angered, the old man changed himself into a huge fish, and when his reluctant wife came to his waterhole to gather lily roots, he devoured her

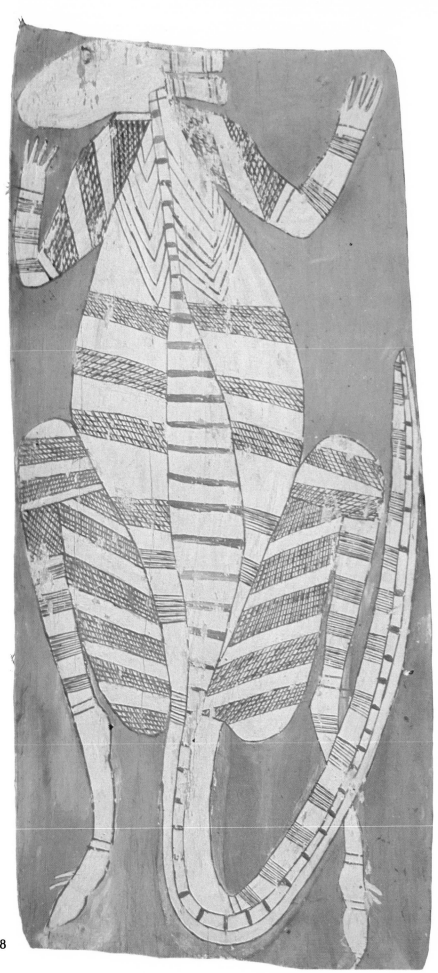

After the Mimis had killed Kundaagi, they cooked his body and ate it, but did not destroy any of the bones. This enabled his mother to bring him back to life. Here Yirawala depicts Kundaagi cooking on the coals

GURGURR, THE MOON MAN

When Yirawala was told the Americans had safely put a man on the moon he shrugged his shoulders and said, 'That not so big thing. My people put man and dog there long, long time ago. I tell you all 'bout it.'

This is the story he told me:

Gurgurr was a man who lived in the Dreamtime. He was travelling a long way with his dog, Mulutji, and they had gone far into the inland and were very thirsty. The dog would run ahead of Gurgurr sniffing for food or water and, finding none, would whine desperately. Suddenly, however, the dog began sniffing at a place in the great hot, dry land, and then started to dig with all his might.

Gurgurr went to the dog, and it nipped him on the neck and whined as it began digging again. Gurgurr bent down and started helping with the digging and soon a trickle of water came to the surface, then a great spout of water burst from the earth, filling the hole and crumbling in the sides until a mighty stream rushed across the land, cutting deeply as it travelled to the distant sea.

Gurgurr and the dog were trapped in the water, trying to stay afloat, but mostly going under as they clung to each other for support and comfort. Gurgurr said: 'Mulutji, we cannot get out of here—we are finished.'

The little dog cried as though agreeing, then Gurgurr added, 'But we will never be forgotten, because when we die our reflections will go to the moon. Men will see us there and remember us always for the water we have brought (now called the Liverpool River), and people will know that this place where we die will remain as a whirlpool in the river.'

And so, to this day, tribal Aborigines are convinced that Gurgurr and his dog, Mulutji, are on the moon looking down at them as a reminder of how a great river was born.

Gurgurr and Mulutji as they
appear on the moon

Far left:
Gurgurr and his dog Mulutji,
trapped in the flood of water they
had released when looking for
water. This swelled to become
the Liverpool River. For bringing
forth this great river, the man
and his dog were immortalized
on the moon

BOOMA-BOOMA, THE BIG MAN

Yirawala explained to me in his distinctive way that the painting he was showing me was a 'proper painting' of Booma-booma, the giant who did everything wrong.

Booma-booma, Yirawala said, was endowed with a huge reproductive organ and delighted stealing young girls whom he would rape. Because of the fear people had for him he lived alone by himself in the bush, and came out only at night when he raided camps to steal girls or babies. He ate the babies.

Yirawala pointed out that there were always plenty of babies for Booma-booma to steal, and it was never hard for him to find them. He just followed the sound of their crying at night.

One night, however, Booma-booma stole and ate the son of Wullur and Wullur vowed he would exact vengeance upon Booma-booma. He painted himself white, threw a spear into the ground and called on his many relatives to help him.

Waving a woomera, Wullur raged against Booma-booma until the other men were just waiting for him to lead them to war against the cruel giant. They set out early one morning towards the jungle where Booma-booma lived and arrived as the sun was high overhead. Wullur told his followers to wait while he went to investigate, and he crept through the dank undergrowth until he heard the sound of snoring. He moved closer and found Booma-booma asleep near the remains of a baby.

Blind rage now filled Wullur. He leapt from cover and struck the giant again and again with his club. The other men heard the sound of battle and raced to help but arrived as Booma-booma rolled over dead.

Wullur and his followers then built a huge fire and threw the giant's body on to it, leaving it to burn. When the men left, the body became a red-hot coal, and the skeleton said, 'My old body is finished now, but I will rise and live again.'

And at that moment the bones took on new flesh, and a two-headed woman crawled from the ashes.

However, even Yirawala could not explain to me the significance of the two-headed woman, except to say, 'it very old story . . . very old.'

The picture shows Yirawala with his painting of Booma-booma as he was supposed to be before being burned and as the two-headed woman he became.

Far left:
Booma-booma. This man was an evil magician who was banished from his tribe for his sins. In vengeance Booma-booma preyed on human babies for food. After he had been killed and burned by the brave Wullur, he came back to life as a two-headed woman

84

NAMORREN, THE LIGHTNING MAN

Long ago, in the Dreaming time, a number of Gunwinggu men were out hunting and stopped to rest near a waterhole. The older men told the younger ones they must not use the waterhole to wash in or something terrible would happen to them.

One young man named Namorul was defiant, and said to himself, 'I am young and stronger than those old men. Nothing can hurt me. I will go and wash the sticky honey from my hands. I am not frightened by these old tales.'

So he went to the pool and washed. Later two young men who were his brothers asked him why he had defied the older men, and they told him they were frightened for him, for what he had done was against tribal law.

Namorul laughed and said, 'Rubbish. Look at me. I am all right. Nothing hurt me because I was not afraid. I am strong, and I did what I wanted to do. That is the only way.'

His brothers told him they were still afraid for him, and that he should listen to what the older men said. But Namorul laughed and walked away.

That night the sky became very dark and a bright streak of lightning came through the night like a giant spear and struck Namorul, severing his head and slicing his body down his backbone to his genitals.

Soon the fate of Namorul was told to all the tribe, and has been passed down the years to young people, especially those who are defiant of older people. Namorren, the Lightning Man, they warn, does not act alone, but is summoned to exact his punishment against wrongdoers by a medicine man who sings him up, and bids him to do his work.

Far left:
Namorren of the lightning

Far right:
Namorul cut to pieces by Namorren for breaking the taboo of the waterhole

85

Maraian designs for body painting. Men of the Dua moiety show the raark design first taught to the people by the Dreaming time giant, Lumah-lumah. The patterns of painted lines represent the slashes the giant cut on his body with a sharp stone just before he died. Lumah-lumah is a primary figure of the Maraian

Maraian designs for body painting, Jiritja moiety

Over page:
The reincarnation of Kundaagi. His mother gathered his bones when the Mimis had finished eating, and sang magic over them to bring her son back to life as a man. It is important to note in all these legends that the Aborigines make little differentiation between human and animal forms when referring to their Dreaming time heroes. Kundaagi's return to life as a man is a statement of belief in an after-life and in the unity of man with nature. Even the tribal kinship classification is extended to include all living and non-living things. The sense of historical unity is strong, too. The Lorrgon mortuary ceremony performed to this day is the very same as that which Kundaagi's mother sang over his bones. Thus, with every death, this belief in an after-life and in man's unity with the physical world is re-affirmed

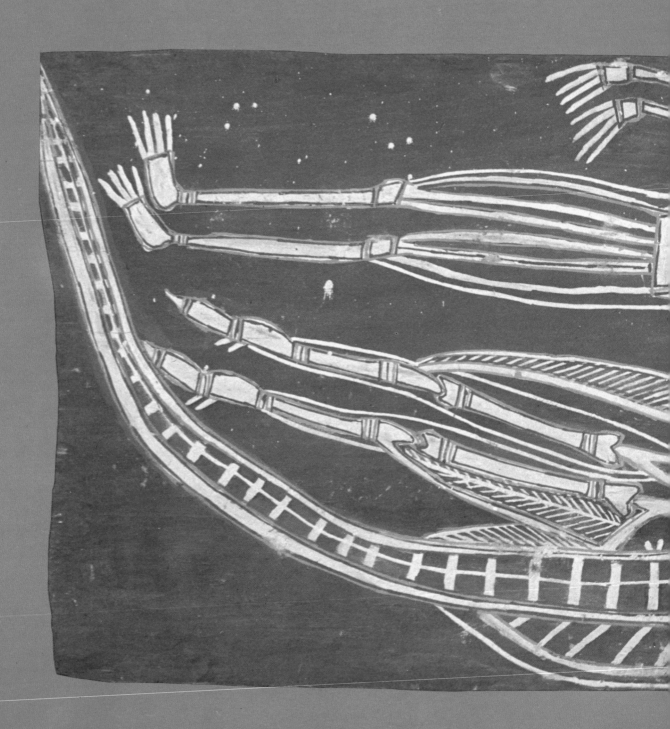

POSTSCRIPT

Yirawala and I subsequently went on a tour of Australia and New Guinea for the Australian Council for the Arts, to give displays of his magnificent works in their ceremonial series and to lecture. The tour was very successful, especially with school children and university students who came to learn as well as to look.

At the University of Papua New Guinea the display and lectures created great interest and enthusiasm. The Papua New Guineans were astonished at the beauty of Yirawala's works and the wisdom of the old artist. They treated him like a king, and asked many questions about 'the Australian men'—meaning, of course, the Aborigines.

One headman came down from the mountains in full regalia to meet and welcome Yirawala and to exchange gifts. Strangely enough, the two men communicated quite well. This also happened with other people of Papua New Guinea, who flocked around Yirawala wherever he went.

Yirawala and various headmen compared notes during a great dance festival at the university, and Yirawala remarked to me (and some of the headmen concurred), that some Aboriginal stories were similar to ones from New Guinea. All said that long ago in some place there must have been contact between Australia and New Guinea.

Yirawala loves New Guinea and its people and I know he will always remember them with deep affection.

At this first Festival of Arts in Papua New Guinea in 1971 the old artist met many people from other countries, but he was most impressed with Mr Segun Olusola from Lagos, Nigeria, who told him of his great country and something of its stories and poetry, and who presented Yirawala with a beautifully made leather bag. Yirawala addressed Mr Olusola as his son, and the two established a bond of true affection for each other. On parting, they vowed to meet again one day.

Later, Yirawala was presented with the M.B.E. for his contribution to art.

Late in December 1971, Yirawala came to Darwin to attend a function of the Royal Commonwealth Society, and decided to stay a few weeks afterwards with me. His stay was marred by a bad fall, and he was hospitalized. I spent hours with him at the hospital, and gradually Yirawala's will to live triumphed. He had sustained a broken right arm and head injuries in the fall, but each week he grew stronger, until the great day when the plaster was taken off his arm. He could walk, and set off home, almost completely restored.

In the meantime I have had to face certain hard financial facts. For years I have been trying to get support in the Northern Territory for a museum to house Yirawala's works, along with tapes and photographic data and an extensive collection of Aboriginal art and artifacts from various areas:

Far left:
The artist's hands. The subject is Kundaagi. Great patience, skill, and knowledge are obvious in each of his works

91

but all to no avail. I even tried renting premises in the city for such a museum, but failed for lack of money. There is still no support here.

In Sydney, a well-to-do businessman reading a newspaper article on the need for a home for the collection, did offer to establish a private museum in Sydney, with no strings attached. This is still under discussion, but not yet finalized.

It has been pointed out to me by experts that the collection, unless stored under proper conditions, must surely deteriorate and ultimately be lost.

When Yirawala recovered from his fall, we discussed the idea of the private museum in Sydney, where his works could be kept for all time and where he and his sons could stay from time to time. He liked the idea very much.

At the time of writing, nothing is resolved for the future, except that I am resolved that the ceremonial series of Yirawala's works will never be broken up.